MW01283837

# THE KETOGENIC VEGETARIAN COOKBOOK

*Fast, Simple, and Delicious Keto Vegetarian Diet Recipes For Rapid Weight Loss*

*Lose Weight, Heal Your Body and Upgrade Your Lifestyle*

# Table of Contents

# Introduction

The ketogenic diet, sometimes referred to as a "keto" diet for short, is a way of eating that takes advantage of your body's metabolic tendencies to produce weight loss and other beneficial biological reactions. A keto diet primarily revolves around a significantly reduced intake of carbohydrates, usually with a corresponding increase in the intake of fats and proteins, so it's sometimes also referred to as a "low carb" or a "low carb/high fat" diet.

It's the reduction in carbs that packs the keto diet's real punch, though, and that's the focus of most keto recipes. Keto recipes eliminate the sources of carbohydrates that make up the bulk of traditional Western diets—grains, breads, pasta, starches, and sugars—and emphasize instead proteins, as well as relatively low-carb vegetables and fruits.

The fact that the ketogenic diet traditionally relies heavily on meats as a source of protein while also limiting plant-based sources of carbohydrates makes it challenging to combine keto and vegetarian diets. Vegetarians have to get creative in order to eliminate meats from their diet, achieve balanced nutrition, and also force their bodies into a state of ketosis.

It's not easy, but it can be done, and this book is designed to help you do it. We'll lay out the principles that underlie both the ketogenic and vegetarian diets, and we'll look for ways that the two approaches to nutrition can work well together. And we'll give you the recipes that will make the combination as effortless and successful as possible.

# The Ketogenic Diet

The ketogenic diet was originally developed as a therapy to improve neurological function in epileptics, but its wide-ranging metabolic and nutritional benefits have led millions to pursue keto programs as part of their complete nutritional plans. While weight loss is not the only benefit of a keto diet, many weight-loss programs are designed to produce a ketogenic phase that helps to shift the body's metabolism into a state more conducive to burning stored fat.

## What is the Ketogenic Diet?

In the strictest sense, a ketogenic diet is a nutritional program that focuses on relatively high fat intake, moderate protein intake, and low carbohydrate intake. The goal of the diet is to force the body to burn fat as fuel rather than carbohydrates, the fuel that the metabolic system leans on most heavily under normal conditions. The hope is that the body will become conditioned to burning fat stores--and thereby kick starting weight loss--rather than relying on carbohydrate fuels and simply storing fat.

### The Beginning of Ketosis

Typically, the human body produces energy by converting carbohydrates in food into glucose and then burning that glucose in its cells. Carbohydrates are relatively easy for the body to convert into glucose, making them an ideal fuel source, and the body's metabolic system will rely on them when it can, fueling itself with carbohydrates as they enter the digestive system from food and leaving stored fat in place.

When excess carbohydrates are consumed, the metabolic system converts any carbs it doesn't need for fuel into fat and stores that fat in the body. Then the body resists burning that stored fat, opting instead to burn freshly consumed carbs, and the cycle starts over again.

However, if sufficient carbohydrates aren't present in a person's diet, the body will be forced to look elsewhere for the energy it needs. The next most preferred fuel source is fat, which is metabolized in the liver. The liver turns fat into fatty acids and other water-soluble molecules called ketone bodies, which can be used in the body's cells as a fuel source. When the liver is actively metabolizing fat and the level of ketone bodies in the blood stream is elevated above typical levels, the body is said to have entered a state of ketosis.

### *Harnessing Ketosis*

The ketogenic diet was originally developed as a therapeutic diet for patients with epilepsy. Research indicated that when patients' brain activity was fueled by ketone bodies instead of by glucose, the frequency of epileptic seizures in study subjects decreased. The therapeutic diet was first developed in the 1920s and although it gradually fell out of favor because of the advent of pharmaceutical therapies for epilepsy, the diet experienced a revival in interest among clinicians in the 1990s. That's when some dietary researchers began to incorporate elements of a ketogenic diet into their low-carbohydrate regimens even for those who were not struggling with epilepsy.

The popular low-carb diets of the 1990s and early 2000s attempted to harness ketosis by guiding adherents through an initial phase during which carbohydrate intake was drastically reduced. The theory was that by producing ketosis through severely limited carb intake, the body would shift to a fat-burning mode, triggering an initial rapid weight loss that could be sustained even when carbohydrate intake was moderately increased later in the program. These approaches also emphasized diets that would inhibit the production of insulin, which aids in the processing of glucose and inhibits the metabolic processing of fats.

## What are the Benefits of a Ketogenic Diet?

### *Weight loss*

The promise of rapid, dramatic weight loss is the lure of the keto diet for many of adherents. It's not uncommon for a keto diet to produce weight loss of several pounds in the first week or so, and it's hard to resist the possibility to such a quick result. Everyone who tries a keto diet will experience something different, however, and consistent, sustained weight loss will only happen when you dedicate careful attention to your food intake and exercise program.

The big initial weight loss that often accompanies the beginning of keto diet is generally attributable to a loss of your body's water content. As you shift the proportion of nutrients you take in, your body will attempt to adjust to the new order of things, and part of that adjustment is typically the release of a significant amount of water. Fluid loss can account for the loss of up to 10 pounds of weight in the first week of a diet.

This initial weight loss is only the beginning, though. The water loss is an indication that your body is changing the way it processes nutrients, and it's the first step in moving your metabolism toward a state of ketosis. As you continue to follow the diet, your weight loss is likely to slow, but the weight loss is theoretically more like to come from the metabolism of stored fat, which is the overall goal of the diet program.

### Blood Sugar Control

Remember how we said that your body can easily convert carbohydrates into fuel? That means that when you eat lots of carbs, your body can very easily turn those carbs into the glucose that your cells can use as fuel. The glucose is transported through your blood stream, so high carbohydrate intake can result in significant spikes in your blood sugar (glucose) level.

A keto diet can help to eliminate spikes in blood sugar levels by giving your body fats and proteins to process instead of carbs. These nutrients are not as readily converted to glucose, so blood sugar spikes are not nearly as likely to occur when you eat more of them and fewer carbs.

### Appetite Control

The flip side to a blood sugar spike is a blood sugar crash that comes after your cells quickly devour the glucose produced by high carbohydrate consumption. Carbs are processed and consumed quickly, leaving your body wanting more after they're all gone. It's a roller coaster ride for your body in terms of energy, and it plays havoc with your appetite. Eat a bunch of carbs and you might feel full in the moment, but you're likely to be hungry again in a ridiculously short time.

A keto diet can help to stabilize your appetite and eliminate cravings by reducing the ups and downs caused by high carb intake. A diet high in fats and proteins can help you to feel full faster and stave off hunger longer than a diet that relies too heavily on carbohydrates.

### Energy Levels

Another benefit of stabilized blood sugar is the stabilization of your energy level throughout the day. When your blood sugar level crashes, you not only get hungry, you also get tired. Without carbs to provide quick and easy energy, your body doesn't think it has anywhere to turn, so it simply gives up and gets lethargic until it convinces you to eat more carbs.

Your body on a keto diet behaves differently. After you've trained your body to enter a state of ketosis, it knows where to look for energy when there are no carbs readily available. There's plenty of energy to be found in your stored fat, and a body that's used to a keto diet is able to utilize that energy to keep you from feeling tired and lethargic even between meals.

### Keto Diet and Insulin Resistance

Insulin is a hormone that allows your body to process glucose. Your body's production of insulin is a natural process that is crucial to controlling the level of glucose in your blood and fueling your cells. Some people, however, develop insulin resistance, which means that insulin becomes less effective at processing glucose in their bodies, leading to elevated blood sugar levels and potentially serious health problems.

A keto diet helps to sidestep the problems of insulin resistance by stabilizing blood sugar levels. Your body becomes less dependent on insulin production, and the impact of insulin resistance is decreased, too.

## What are Carbohydrates, Fats and Proteins?

Now you know how a keto diet works to help your body to process fats, proteins and carbohydrates, but to fully understand the benefits of keto, you need to understand what fats, proteins and carbs are in the first place.

Fats, proteins, and carbohydrates are compounds called macronutrients. They are categories of substances that fuel our metabolic processes, and we need large amounts of them in order to live. In various combinations, these three types of macronutrients make up most of the foods we eat.

Carbohydrates (or "carbs" for short) make up the bulk of the foods in the typical Western diet. They are chemical compounds that contain carbon, hydrogen, and oxygen, and as we have already learned, they're easily processed by the body into cell-fueling glucose. Common carbohydrates include the fructose sugar in fruits, the lactose sugar in dairy products, and the sucrose in common table sugar. The starches and cellulose in vegetables are also carbohydrates.

Proteins are compounds made up of chains of amino acids. They are not as easily used by the body for fuel, but they are vital for other cell functions, maintenance, and repair. In our diet, proteins primarily come from animal products such as meat or eggs, but they can also be found in some plant-based foods such as nuts and legumes.

Fats are compounds consisting of chains of fatty acids. As a nutrient, fats are an excellent source of energy, but under typical metabolic conditions, they're more often used as a way to store energy for later use. Fatty acids are stored in specialized tissues in the body, and they're only used for energy when necessary. In the diet, fats can come from either animal or plant sources.

## How is a Ketogenic Diet Structured?

Remember that the goal of a keto diet is to force your body into a state of ketosis. That's when your body has begun metabolizing fat in your liver and producing ketone bodies to help fuel your cells. Your body will only enter a state of ketosis when it has to; as long as it has an adequate supply of easy-to-use carbohydrates at its disposal, it will continue burning them. When it runs out of carbs, it will simply demand more by making you hungry. It will not, however, work very hard to burn stored fat.

If, however, you convince your body that no more carbs are on the way, it will have no choice but to resort to ketosis and start burning fat. The only way that's going to happen is if you severely limit your intake of carbohydrates and correspondingly increase your intake of the other two macronutrients.

The ideal ratio of macronutrients for a keto diet will vary from person to person depending on factors such as age, weight, body fat percentage, and activity level. However, some general goals can help you to structure your diet to give you the best chance of pushing your body into a state of ketosis.

First of all, and most importantly, your diet must include a very low proportion of carbohydrates. In most cases, carbohydrates shouldn't make up more than five percent of the macronutrients you consume, and even lower levels of carb consumption are sometimes necessary. This is virtually the opposite of the mainstream Western diet and often the hardest part of the keto diet to pull off.

Keto diets usually include a moderate intake of proteins, generally somewhere between 15 and 35 percent of all the macronutrients you take in. It's important to maintain moderate protein consumption, because low protein intake can lead to situations that undermine the benefits of the keto diet.

Fats typically make up the majority of macronutrients in a keto diet, with the proportion usually falling between 60 and 80 percent. The goal is to transform fats into your body's primary fuel source, so you need lots of them.

With each recipe in this book, we've included an estimate of the amount of carbohydrates, fats, and protein in the finished dishes. These numbers are estimates only—the actual nutrient content of the dishes will vary depending on the specifics of the ingredients and how they're prepared—but you can use them as a starting point for planning your diet.

### The Best Keto Foods

When you're on a keto diet, foods high in fats and protein are your friend, although you should look for the healthiest versions of these foods. You can safely eat meats, fish, poultry, and eggs. There are also plenty of plant-based fats that fit well into a keto diet, including olive oil, coconut oil, and avocado. You can also feel good about eating most leafy vegetables and greens.

Other foods that contain a balance of carbohydrates, fats and proteins should be eaten less often but can still be part of a keto diet. These foods include dairy products, nuts, root vegetables, cabbage, cauliflower, broccoli, tomatoes, peppers, and mushrooms.

### Foods to Avoid on the Ketogenic Diet

To make a keto diet successful, you have to steer clear of foods that are high in carbohydrates. That means you need to avoid grains and foods made from them (including breads, pasta, and rice), legumes (like beans and peas), starchy vegetables (potatoes, carrots, corn), sugars (including honey and syrups), and most fruits.

This doesn't mean you can never eat any of these foods, but you have to be very aware of their relatively high carbohydrate content. You're best staying away from bread altogether, but occasionally including beans or peas in your dishes can be acceptable.

# What are the Dangers of the Ketogenic Diet?

A keto diet has many benefits, but in some rare cases, it can have some side effects. Before you embark on a keto program, you should be aware of its potential pitfalls.

### Ketoacidosis

Ketoacidosis is a potentially very serious metabolic condition that results from a combination of high ketone levels and high blood sugar levels in the bloodstream. It is most often a complication of type 1 diabetes, and it is very rare in people without diabetes. However, because the name of the condition is so similar to the state of ketosis encouraged by a keto diet, the two states are often confused. In reality, healthy people should have no reason to be concerned that a keto diet will trigger ketoacidosis.

### Keto Flu

As you begin the keto diet, you will be pushing your body to change the way it fuels itself. As you shift from a carbohydrate fuel source to the fat fuel source used during ketosis, you're likely to encounter an interim period during which your body isn't quite sure where it should look for fuel.

During this time before ketosis really kicks in, some people experience lethargy, grogginess, or other minor ill feelings. Sometimes referred to as "keto flu," this unpleasant effect will almost always dissipate in just a few days as your body adjusts to the diet.

### Constipation

Constipation is a common problem among people who are new to the keto diet. The problem is likely caused by the loss of fluid triggered by the sudden change in diet, as well as the likelihood that you're eating less fiber in a low-carb diet. The solution is usually to be sure that you're drinking plenty of water and eating leafy vegetables that contain a relatively high amount of fiber.

### Low Physical Performance

Athletes are often concerned that a low-carb diet will result in reduced athletic performance since their bodies are trained to use carbohydrates as their main energy source. If your athletic activity requires you to perform at high intensity for a short time, you might experience a degradation in your performance while you're on a keto diet.

While that might be true for athletes who need high energy levels for short bursts of time, endurance athletes know that being able to tap into fat stores for energy can actually increase performance. During endurance sports such as distance running, performance increases when an athlete is able to access energy in stored fat after readily available carbs are gone.

# The Vegetarian Diet

In the simplest sense, a vegetarian diet is a program of nutrition that relies entirely on plant-based foods and limits or eliminates, to some degree, food products that are derived from animals. People pursue vegetarian diets for a variety of reasons and to varying degrees of completeness, but all vegetarian diets share at least some rejection of animal-based foods in favor of other nutrition sources.

The most common way to classify different kinds of vegetarian diets is to focus on the extent to which they eliminate animal food sources. There are five common types of vegetarian diet that are widely practiced.

### The Lacto-Vegetarian Diet

This vegetarian diet eliminates all kinds of meat, including foods made from fish, shellfish and poultry, as well as red meats. It also eliminates foods that contain or are derived from meats, including stocks and broths.

The lacto-vegetarian diet, however, does allow the consumption of dairy products, including milk, cheese, yogurt, and butter. It also allows products that are derived from or contain dairy products. The inclusion of dairy products in the diet provides a source of animal-based protein, but it sidesteps the ethical issues that come from consuming meat, which require the death of the animal from which it comes.

### The Ovo-Vegetarian Diet

The ovo-vegetarian diet, like the lacto-vegetarian diet, excludes all kinds of meat, including fish, shellfish and poultry. It also excludes dairy products. It does allow, however, the consumption of eggs and foods that are made from or contain eggs.

Like the lacto-vegetarian diet, the ovo-vegetarian diet takes advantage of animal protein sources but avoids those that are lethal to the animal. Often, the elimination of dairy products comes about as a rejection of the ethical problems surrounding the industrial dairy industry. The possibility of more humane and sustainable egg production, however, addresses those issues and provides a rationale for continuing to include eggs in the diet.

### The Lacto-Ovo-Vegetarian Diet

As is probably obvious from the name, the lacto-ovo-vegetarian diet excludes meat, but it allows both dairy products and eggs. The goal here is to eliminate the problems associated with meat consumption, both ethical and nutritional, while still allowing less problematic access to animal proteins.

A lacto-ovo-vegetarian diet is quite flexible, relatively, compared to other vegetarian diets. The inclusion of milk, eggs, cheese, butter and eggs, along with their derivatives, gives the practitioner the ability to easily add protein from a variety of sources to their diet, and the list of excluded foods is clear-cut and relatively easy to understand.

### The Pescatarian Diet

This largely vegetarian diet eliminates almost all sources of animal proteins, including meat, poultry, dairy products and eggs, but it allows the consumption of fish and, usually, other types of seafood. Sometimes the rationale for this diet involves a perceived difference in the ethical problems between consuming fish and other meats, but it's more often a result of a desire to replace nutritionally problematic meats with more healthy fish and seafood.

Less common is the pollotarian diet, which allows the consumption of poultry but eliminates meat, fish, dairy products and eggs.

### The Vegan Diet

This diet is the most restrictive of the vegetarian diets. A vegan diet totally excludes all sources of food products derived from animals. It excludes meat, fish, seafood, poultry, dairy products and eggs, as well as all food products that contain any animal products or that are derived from them.

## Benefits of the Vegetarian Diet

By removing meats and other animal products from a practitioner's nutritional program, the vegetarian diet offers a variety of health diets, mostly from the elimination of things that may be harmful to overall health in both the short term and the long term. Ethical and environmental concerns aside, a vegetarian diet may also make a dieter healthier in the long run.

Excluding meat, especially red meat, from the diet may reduce the consumption of certain nutrients that can increase the risk of health problems such as heart disease or cancer. Eliminating animal products also has the benefit of getting rid of chemical additives, such as growth hormones, that are used during the industrial production of animal products; these substances may also have adverse health effects when consumed over time.

By not eating food sources that sit high on the food chain, vegetarians also reduce their exposure to environmental contaminants that tend to become more concentrated in food sources higher on the food chain. Contaminants that already exist in the environment or that are used in industrial food production may be absorbed by plants, and as animals (such as cows and pigs) eat these plants, the contaminants are absorbed in greater concentrations by those animals. In cases where humans eat predator animals that eat other animals (such as many species of fish), the concentration of contaminants in the food source becomes even greater. Choosing sources of food that are low on the food chain--plants--minimizes this problem.

Finally, a vegetarian diet can be, if pursued correctly, a great tool for weight loss. Because animal products, especially red meats and full-fat dairy products, are relatively high in calorie-dense fats, foods that contain these animal products tend to have many more calories than comparable foods made from plant-based products. By removing high-calorie animal products from the diet, the dieter is more easily able to reduce their overall caloric intake and thereby lose weight.

## Drawbacks of the Vegetarian Diet

Vegetarian diets have many benefits, but they're not perfect. If they're not structured correctly, they can lead to nutritional deficiencies, and in the worst cases, they may be even less healthful than a non-restrictive diet.

Humans have evolved to function best on an omnivorous diet, meaning that they are designed to consume both plant- and animal-based food sources. Unlike herbivores like cows, which can subsist happily eating only plants, or carnivores like cats, which can get by just fine without ever eating plants at all, humans need a range of nutrients, some which are found only in plants and some of which are found only in animals. Because of this, constructing a diet from only plant sources has the potential to create problems that have to be managed mindfully.

## Processed Foods

It's not always easy to follow a vegetarian diet, or any restrictive diet for that matter. Choosing foods that fit within the diet's restrictions takes time, effort, and thought, and often vegetarian dishes are more labor-intensive to prepare than simple meat-based dishes.

As a result, vegetarians sometimes rely too heavily on processed vegetarian foods. These processed foods may eliminate animal products, but they often are relatively high in other ingredients that are less than healthy. Producers may take the easy way out in replacing the flavor lost through the elimination of animal fats by boosting the amount of salt, sugars, or plant-based fats in their processed products. Preservatives, additives and other chemical components are also often over-represented in these products, making them even less healthy overall than carefully chosen meat products.

## Calcium

Calcium is an essential nutrient that helps maintain healthy teeth and bones. For those on non-restricted diets, the most common sources of dietary calcium are milk and other dairy products. Lacto-vegetarians are still able to access these sources of calcium, but other vegetarians and vegans are at risk of eating a diet that's deficient in calcium. The potential solution is to eat plenty of dark green vegetables, which are relatively rich in calcium. Another option is to eat processed foods that are artificially fortified with calcium or to take a calcium supplement.

## Vitamin D

Vitamin D is also crucial in the develop of healthy bones. It is unique among nutrients in that the human body can produce vitamin D when it is exposed to sunlight. Not everyone gets enough daily sun exposure to produce an adequate amount of vitamin D, however, so the nutrient is commonly added to cow's milk. Therefore, a vegetarian who excludes dairy products and also doesn't get much sun exposure is in danger of being vitamin-D deficient. The answer, again, is to consume fortified food or take a dietary supplement.

## Vitamin B12

Vitamin B12 is used in the production of red blood cells, so it is a critically important nutritional component. Unfortunately for vegetarians, it's found almost exclusively in animal products. Lacto-ovo-vegetarians may not be at risk of vitamin B12 deficiency, but vegans certainly are. Once again, fortified foods or supplements are the best solution.

## Iron

Iron, also, is necessary for the production of healthy red blood cells, and it is found in relatively large quantities in animal products. In vegetarian diets, it can be found in legumes, whole grains and fruits. The problem is that these plant-based food sources are generally limited in the ketogenic diet, so vegetarians who are pursuing a keto plan must be careful to get enough iron.

## Protein

Perhaps the single largest challenge for vegetarians is the consumption of enough protein. This macronutrient is essential for good health, and its most readily accessible source in the diet is meat.

There are, however, other good sources of protein that can easily replace the protein in meat. Eggs are an excellent source of protein, so ovo-vegetarians have little to worry about. Other vegetarians can look to legumes, whole grains, nuts and seeds for protein.

# Important Foods for Vegetarians

Because of the above-mentioned nutritional concerns, vegetarians need to be careful to choose the right foods to include in their nutrition plans. With good planning, a vegetarian diet can be nutritionally complete and just as healthy, if not more so, than a non-restrictive diet.

Vegetarians can do well by leaning toward colorful vegetables, which tend to be dense in vitamins and other nutrients. Dark green, leafy vegetables should be a large part of the diet, and red and orange fruits and vegetables should be an even larger part.

Whole grains, seeds, nuts and legumes deliver many different kinds of essential nutrients, including dietary fiber, protein, fats, amino acids and protein.

Foods to avoid whenever possible include processed grains, excess sodium, added sugars, saturated and trans fats, and other refined carbohydrates.

# Combing the Ketogenic and Vegetarian Diets

Putting these two diets together offers great opportunities, but it also presents significant challenges. Combining the weight loss potential of ketosis with the inherently low-calorie content of the vegetarian diet means that weight loss can be even easier to achieve than it is with either diet alone. Also, the restrictions of both diets may complement each other, allowing you to eliminate most the unhealthy foods in your diet and to focus on the most healthy ones.

The combination requires some work, though. In some ways, the restrictions of the keto and vegetarian diets contradict each other. The keto diet aims to ramp up the diet's protein and fat content while substantially curtailing the carbohydrate content. To do so, it traditionally relies on meat, which is relatively high in both fat and protein and low in carbs. That's a problem for a vegetarian dieter.

Conversely, the vegetarian diet needs to make up for lost protein when it eliminates meat. To do so, it traditionally increases the dieter's intake of whole grains and legumes, some of the best sources of non-animal proteins. These foods, however, are generally severely limited in the keto diet because they are relatively high in carbohydrates. This, too, is a problem.

To get around these problems, the keto-vegetarian dieter has to be a creative meal planner. You have to find the places where the two diets intersect and choose the foods that will give you complete nutrition while also fulfilling the goals of both diets. Fortunately, there are plenty of food choices that will do just that.

## Foods for the Ketogenic Vegetarian Diet

The list of foods that you should choose on this combined diet should be low in carbohydrates, but they should also be good sources of the nutrients that are at risk of being lacking in a vegetarian diet.

## Protein Sources

If you're a lacto-ovo vegetarian, this one is easy for you. Dairy products and eggs can easily replace the protein you'll lose by eliminating meats, and they're also low in carbs (especially eggs).

If you're not able to eat dairy products or eggs, look to seeds (chia, flax, hemp, etc.) and nuts (almonds, walnuts) for proteins. Whole sources of these foods are great, but also consider nut butters and milks and seed meals.

## Amino Acids, Calcium, Iron and Vitamin D

Again, seeds and nuts are your friends when it comes to finding these nutrients. Dark green, leafy vegetables like kale and spinach can help, too, as can soy-based products.

## Ask Your Doctor

As is the case with any diet or nutrition program, a keto diet isn't for everyone. While it delivers measurable benefits for most people, the keto diet depends on a dramatic shift away from the typical balance of dietary nutrients, and such a dramatic shift can exacerbate some existing health conditions and may trigger others.

Before you begin a keto diet—or any other diet, for that matter—you should always consult with a doctor or other medical professional to be sure that it's safe for you to alter your food intake in the ways demanded by the keto. You should also pay close attention to how your body is responding to the diet as you progress, and if something doesn't feel right, consult your doctor.

Because the combination of a ketogenic diet and a vegetarian diet can be so nutritionally complex, it's a great idea to consult with a licensed nutrition or dietitian before you embark on such a plan. A consultation will help you to be sure that you're getting adequate nutrition, and it can help you to have the right foods on hand to be able to properly stick to the plan.

# Recipes

Following a ketogenic diet requires you to make some big changes to the way you eat, and that can be a challenge, especially for busy people who don't have the time to learn a whole new way of cooking and meal planning. The problem is made even more challenging when you throw in the restrictions of a vegetarian diet, which introduces a whole new set of concerns and limitations.

We've tried to collect recipes that will satisfy the requirements of a range of diets. Some of the recipes take advantage of dairy products and eggs as sources of protein, but there are also plenty of recipes that are entirely free of animal products and that will respect the requirements of strict vegetarians and vegans. None of the recipes include meat, fish or poultry, and all of them adhere to the nutritional guidelines of the ketogenic diet.

The recipes we've included here are full of flavor and variety. They get the most from the limitations of the keto and vegetarian diets, allowing you to have a new keto-friendly dish every day of the week if you want. Best of all, the simplicity of the recipes ensures that anyone, no matter how pressed for time, can fit a keto diet into their lifestyle.

# Breakfast

A keto diet has plenty of room in it for classic breakfast foods like eggs, but your keto breakfast doesn't have to stick to the boring basics. If you're not an ovo-vegetarian, breakfast is even more of a conundrum, but we're looking out for you by including some protein-rich, egg-free breakfast dishes. These recipes will give you new twists on old favorites so you can start every day in a keto way.

## *Egg Scramble*

**Servings:** 6
**Time Required:** About 4.5 hours
**Ingredients:**

- 1 onion, diced
- 2 cups cheddar cheese, grated
- 10 eggs
- 1 cup whole milk
- 1 tsp. salt
- 1 tsp. pepper

**Directions:**

1. Put the onion and cheese into the slow cooker.
2. In a mixing bowl, whisk together the milk and eggs until the eggs are beaten. Add salt and pepper and stir to mix thoroughly.
3. Poor the egg mixture over the ingredients in a slow cooker.
4. Cover the pot and cook on low for 4 hours.
5. Serve hot.

**Nutrition Information Per Serving:**

- Total Fat: 11 grams
- Carbohydrates: 3 grams
- Protein: 11 grams

### *Pressure Cooker Soft-Boiled Eggs*

**Servings:** 6

**Time Required:** About 10 minutes

**Ingredients:**

- 6 large eggs
- ¾ cup water

**Directions:**

- Put the steamer rack into your pressure cooker and pour in the water.
- Place eggs, still in the shell, on top of the steamer rack.
- Cover and lock the pot.
- Using the Steam function, set the cook time to 2 minutes.
- When the cook time is up, remove the eggs and serve hot.

**Nutrition Information Per Serving:**

- Total Fat: 5 grams
- Carbohydrates: 0 gram
- Protein: 6 grams

## *Keto Hot Breakfast Cereal*

**Servings:** 1

**Time Required:** About 10 minutes

**Ingredients:**

- 2 Tbsp. coconut flour
- 3 Tbsp. golden flaxseed meal
- 1 ½ cups unsweetened almond milk
- Sugar-free sweetener to taste

**Directions:**

1. In a bowl mix together the flour and flaxseed meal.
2. Add to a small sauce pan and stir in the almond milk. Cook over medium heat until it begins to thicken.
3. Once the mixture has begun to thicken, stir in the sweetener to taste (approximately ½ tsp.).

**Nutrition Information Per Serving:**

- Total Fat: 13 grams
- Carbohydrates: 6 grams
- Protein: 18 grams

## *Omelets in a Cup*

**Servings:** 4
**Time Required:** About 20 minutes
**Ingredients:**

- 4 eggs
- ½ cup onion, diced
- ½ cup bell pepper, diced
- ½ cup cheddar cheese, grated
- ¼ cup half and half

**Directions:**

1. In a mixing bowl, whisk together all ingredients until the eggs are beaten and everything is well combined. Season with salt and pepper.
2. Divide the mixture between four small canning jars. Loosely screw the lids onto the jars.
3. Place a steamer rack in a double boiler/steamer and pour 2 cups water into the pot.
4. Place the jars on the steamer rack.
5. Cover the pot.
6. Bring water to a boil and steam for 10 minutes.
7. Remove the jars from the pot and serve the eggs in the jars.

**Nutrition Information Per Serving**

- Total Fat: 9 grams
- Carbohydrates: 2 grams
- Protein: 9 grams

# *Cauliflower Waffles*

**Servings:** 1
**Time Required:** About 25 minutes
**Ingredients:**

- ½ large head cauliflower, riced
- 1 cup mozzarella cheese, finely shredded
- 1 cup collard greens
- 1/3 cup Parmesan cheese
- 2 large eggs
- 2 stalks green onion
- 1 Tbsp. sesame seeds
- 1 Tbsp. olive oil
- 2 tsp. fresh chopped thyme
- 1 tsp. garlic powder
- ½ tsp. ground black pepper
- ½ teaspoon salt

**Directions:**

1. Cut the cauliflower into florets, slice the spring onion, and pull the thyme leaves from their stems.
2. Rice the cauliflower in a food processor, using the pulse mode until the cauliflower is ground into a coarse, crumbly texture.
3. Add the spring onion, thyme and collard greens to the food processor and continue pulsing until everything is well combined.
4. Transfer to a large mixing bowl.
5. Add the mozzarella cheese, Parmesan cheese, eggs, sesame seeds, olive oil, garlic powder, black pepper, and salt.
6. Mix to form a loose batter.
7. Preheat a waffle iron, and when the iron is hot, spoon in the batter. Cook until the waffles are beginning to brown.
8. Serve hot.

**Nutrition Information Per Serving:**

- Total Fat: 15 grams
- Carbohydrates: 6 grams
- Protein: 15 grams

## *Pressure Cooker Keto Yogurt*

**Servings:** 6
**Time Required:** About 10 hours
**Ingredients:**
- ½ gallon whole milk
- 2 Tbsp. yogurt with live yogurt cultures

**Directions:**
1. Pour milk into an electronic pressure cooker with a Yogurt setting.
2. Press the Yogurt button and adjust the mode to the "boil" setting.
3. Stir the milk regularly as it slowly comes to a boil to evenly distribute heat through the liquid.
4. During this process, fill a large container (large enough to hold the pot liner) or sink with ice water.
5. When the pressure cooker indicates that the yogurt boil cycle is finished, check the temperature of the milk with a thermometer. If the milk is not yet at 180 degrees Fahrenheit, run the cycle again.
6. Once the milk is at 180 degrees, carefully remove the pot liner and place it in the ice-water bath. Using the thermometer, keep an eye on the milk's temperature until it reaches 110 degrees.
7. At this point, put the liner back into the pressure cooker.
8. Put the 2 tablespoons of active yogurt in a small bowl and slowly add about 3 tablespoons of the warm milk from the pot. This step tempers the yogurt so that the yogurt cultures survive the transfer to the warm milk.
9. Stir the yogurt into the milk in the pot after it's tempered.
10. Cover and look the pot.
11. Push the Yogurt button and adjust the mode to "normal." Set the cook time to at least 10 hours. The longer the yogurt is processed, the less sweet it will be.
12. After 10 hours, the milk should be transformed into a much thicker yogurt. At this stage, remove the pot liner and place it in the refrigerator for about 4 hours.
13. If you'd like a thicker Greek-style yogurt, line a colander with cheese cloth and place it in a large bowl. Put the yogurt into the colander and allow the liquid whey to drain from the yogurt into the bowl.
14. When the yogurt is at the desired consistency, refrigerate it or serve it immediately.

**Nutrition Information Per Serving:**

- Total Fat: 4 grams
- Carbohydrates: 8 grams
- Protein: 20 grams

# *Flax Seed Cereal*

**Servings:** 6
**Time Required:** About 90 minutes
**Ingredients:**

- ½ cup milled flax seed
- ½ cup hulled hemp seeds
- 2 Tbsp. ground cinnamon
- ½ cup apple juice
- 1 Tbsp. coconut oil

**Directions:**

1. Preheat oven to 300 degrees Fahrenheit.
2. Combine the dry ingredients in a blender or food processor. Add apple juice and coconut oil and blend until the mixture is thoroughly blended and moderately smooth.
3. Spread the batter about 1/16-inch thick on a parchment-lined baking sheet.
4. Bake on the oven's center rack for 15 minutes. Lower the heat to 250 degrees and bake for another 10 minutes.
5. Remove the sheet from the oven and cut the baked cereal into ½-inch squares. A pizza cutter works well for this.
6. Return the baking sheet to the oven and turn off the heat. Keep the sheet in the oven with the door closed for about an hour. At this point, the cereal should be nice and crisp.
7. Serve with almond milk or other non-dairy milk.

**Nutrition Information Per Serving:**

- Total Fat: 9 grams
- Carbohydrates: 1 gram
- Protein: 5 grams

# *Mini Mushroom Keto Quiche*

**Servings:** 6
**Time Required:** About 20 minutes
**Ingredients:**

- ½ cup Swiss cheese, grated
- ¼ cup fresh mushrooms, chopped
- ¼ cup spring onion, diced
- 4 eggs
- ¼ cup milk
- 1 cup water

**Directions:**

1. Using a silicone or heat-proof egg tray, divide the cheese evenly between the cups in the tray, pressing the cheese into the bottom of the cups.
2. Divide the mushrooms and onions among the cups, placing them on top of the cheese.
3. Combine eggs with in a food processor or blender. Season with salt and pepper. Blend until the ingredients are well combined and smooth, about 30 seconds to a minute. Pour the mixture into the cups on top of the cheese, mushrooms and onions.
4. Place the steamer rack in a steamer pot and add the water.
5. Carefully place the tray on top of the steamer rack.
6. Cover the pot.
7. Bring the water to a boil and steam for 15 minutes.
8. After a few minutes of cooling, pop the mini quiches out of the tray and serve immediately.

**Nutrition Information Per Serving**

- Total Fat: 8 grams
- Carbohydrates: 3 grams
- Protein: 9 grams

## *Egg Crepes*

**Servings:** 4
**Time Required:** About 15 minutes
**Ingredients:**

- 6 eggs
- 5 oz. cream cheese, softened
- 1 tsp. cinnamon
- 1 Tbsp. sugar-free sweetener
- 1 Tbsp. butter (for sautéing)

*Filling ingredients:*

- 8 Tbsp. butter, softened
- 1/3 cup sugar-free sweetener
- 1 Tbsp. cinnamon

**Directions:**

1. Blend the first four ingredients together in a blender until smooth. Let the batter rest for 5 minutes.
2. Heat 1 tablespoon butter in a nonstick pan on medium heat.
3. Pour batter into the pan to form a thin layer about 6 inches in diameter. Cook for about 2 minutes, then flip and cook for an additional minute.
4. Remove the crepe and place on a warm plate. Repeat until the batter is gone. It should yield about 8 crepes.
5. Mix sweetener and cinnamon in a small bowl.
6. Stir half of the mixture into the softened butter until smooth.
7. Spread 1 tablespoon of the mixture onto the center of each crepe.
8. Roll up the crepe and sprinkle it with the sweetener and cinnamon mixture.

**Nutrition Information Per Serving:**

- Total Fat: 42 grams
- Carbohydrates: 2 grams
- Protein: 12 grams

# Soups

Many of these recipes are designed with the ultimate convenience in mind, and whenever possible, we've gone with a fix-it-and-forget it approach. With many of these soup and stew recipes, all you'll have to do is dump the ingredients into the pot, get a good simmer going, and sit back and wait for the deliciousness. In a remarkably short time, you'll have a delightful keto-compliant soup. That doesn't mean, though, that you'll have an *ordinary* soup. We've included a range of recipes that draw on the spices and ingredients of international cuisines to keep your keto menu exciting.

## *Creamy Squash Soup*

**Servings:** 10
**Time Required:** About 40 minutes
**Ingredients:**

- 10 cups butternut squash, cubed
- 1 Tbsp. olive oil
- 1 onion, chopped
- 4 cloves garlic, minced
- 1 ½ tsp. salt
- ½ tsp. black pepper
- 5 cups vegetable stock
- 1 cup heavy cream

**Directions:**

1. Heat the oil in a heavy skillet over medium-high heat. Add onion, garlic, salt and pepper and sauté, stirring, until the onion is translucent.
2. Add squash and stock to a large pot. Transfer vegetables to the pot.
3. Bring to a low simmer and cook until the squash is tender, about 20-30 minutes. Add water if necessary during cooking.
4. Add the cream, stirring to combine. If you have an immersion blender, use it to puree the soup in the pot. If not, transfer the soup to a blender or food processor and blend to a smooth puree.
5. Serve warm.

**Nutrition Information Per Serving:**

- Total Fat: 22 grams
- Carbohydrates: 9 grams
- Protein: 3 grams

## *Cauliflower Cheese Soup*

**Servings:** 4
**Time Required:** About 40 minutes
**Ingredients:**

- 1 head cauliflower, chopped
- ½ onion, chopped
- 2 Tbsp. olive oil
- 3 cups chicken stock
- 1 tsp. garlic powder
- 1 tsp. kosher salt
- 4 oz. cream cheese, cubed
- 1 cup cheddar cheese, grated
- ½ cup milk

**Directions:**

1. Heat the oil in a heavy stock pot over medium-high heat. Add onion and cook until softened, about 3 minutes.
2. Add cauliflower, stock, salt and garlic powder.
3. Bring to a low simmer and cook until the cauliflower is tender, about 20 minutes. Add water if necessary during cooking.
4. Transfer cauliflower to a blender or food processor and blend to a smooth puree.
5. Return pureed cauliflower to the pot and add the cream cheese and cheddar cheese, stirring as the mixture heats over medium-low heat.
6. When the cheese has melted, add the milk and heat thoroughly.

**Nutrition Information Per Serving:**

- Total Fat: 8 grams
- Carbohydrates: 17 grams
- Protein: 5 grams

## *Keto Vegetarian Chili*

**Servings:** 10
**Time Required:** About 50 minutes
**Ingredients:**

- 2 ½ lbs. ground beef, 85 percent lean
- ½ large white onion, diced
- 8 cloves garlic, minced
- 2 cans (15 oz. each) diced tomatoes, liquid reserved
- 6 oz. tomato paste
- 4 oz. canned green chilis, liquid reserved
- 2 Tbsp. Worcestershire sauce
- ¼ cup chili powder
- 2 Tbsp. cumin
- 1 Tbsp. dried oregano
- 2 tsp. kosher salt
- 1 tsp. freshly ground black pepper
- 1 Tbsp. olive oil

**Directions:**

1. Heat the oil in a heavy stock pot over medium-high heat. When the oil is hot, add the onions and sauté until soft and translucent, about 5 minutes.
2. Add garlic to the pot and sauté for one minute more.
3. Add the rest of the ingredients to the pot and stir to combine.
4. Bring to a low simmer and cook until fragrant, about 30 minutes. Add water if necessary during cooking.

**Nutrition Information Per Serving:**

- Total Fat: 18 grams
- Carbohydrates: 13 grams
- Protein: 23 grams

# *Keto Mexican-Style Soup*

**Servings:** 8-10
**Time Required:** About 50 minutes
**Ingredients:**

- ¼ cup onion, diced
- 4 cloves garlic, minced
- 2 Tbsp. chili powder
- 2 tsp. cumin
- 20 oz. canned diced tomatoes
- 4 oz. canned green chilis
- 32 oz. beef stock
- 8 oz. cream cheese
- ½ cup heavy cream
- 1 Tbsp. olive oil

**Directions:**

1. Heat the oil in a heavy stock pot over medium-high heat. When the oil is hot, add the onions to the pot and sauté until soft and translucent, about 5 minutes.
2. Add garlic to the pot and sauté for one minute more.
3. Add ground beef to the pot and sauté until the meat is thoroughly browned, stirring constantly with a wooden spoon or spatula. This should take about 10 minutes.
4. Add the rest of the ingredients, excluding the cream and cream cheese, to the pot and stir to combine.
5. Bring to a low simmer and cook until fragrant, about 30 minutes. Add water if necessary during cooking.
6. Stir in cream and cream cheese, stirring constantly until cream cheese is melted and soup is thick and creamy.
7. Transfer to serving bowls and serve hot.

**Nutrition Information Per Serving:**

- Total Fat: 28 grams
- Carbohydrates: 8 grams
- Protein: 27 grams

# *Keto Chinese-Style Soup*

**Servings:** 8-10

**Time Required:** About 40 minutes

**Ingredients:**

- 5 cups vegetable stock
- 1 lb. pork tenderloin or other lean pork, sliced into thin bite-sized pieces
- 1 cup fresh mushrooms, chopped
- 3 Tbsp. soy sauce
- 1 Tbsp. white vinegar
- 2 Tbsp. rice vinegar
- 1 tsp. salt
- 2 tsp. freshly ground black pepper
- 3 Tbsp. water
- 4 eggs, beaten
- 1 lb. tofu, extra firm, cubed

**Directions:**

1. Put all ingredients, excluding eggs and tofu, in a heavy stock pot.
2. Bring to a low simmer and cook until the meat is thoroughly cooked and the mushrooms are tender, about 30 minutes. Add water if necessary during cooking.
3. Slowly and carefully stir in the tofu and beaten eggs. Allow the warm soup to sit for at least 3 minute to allow the eggs to cook.
4. Transfer to serving bowls and serve hot.

**Nutrition Information Per Serving:**

- Total Fat: 5 grams
- Carbohydrates: 5 grams
- Protein: 20 grams

# *Creamy Keto Broccoli Cheese Soup*

**Servings:** 8-10
**Time Required:** About 40 minutes
**Ingredients:**

- 1 cup broccoli, chopped
- 5 oz. cheddar cheese, grated
- 2 Tbsp. butter
- ¼ cup onion, diced
- ¼ cup celery, diced
- 1 ½ cups vegetable stock
- ½ cup heavy cream
- 1 Tbsp. olive oil

**Directions:**

1. Heat the oil in a heavy stock pot over medium-high heat. When the oil is hot, add the onions and celery to the pot and sauté until the onion is soft and translucent, about 5 minutes.
2. Add garlic to the pot and sauté for one minute more.
3. Add the rest of the ingredients, excluding the cream and cheese, to the pot and stir to combine.
4. Bring to a low simmer and cook until the vegetables are tender, about 30 minutes. Add water if necessary during cooking.
5. Stir in cream, stirring constantly until the cheese is melted and soup is thick and creamy.
6. Transfer to serving bowls and serve hot.

**Nutrition Information Per Serving:**

- Total Fat: 36 grams
- Carbohydrates: 5 grams
- Protein: 13 grams

# *Keto Yellow Curry*

**Servings:** 6-8

**Time Required:** About 40 minutes

**Ingredients:**

- 14.5 oz. can unsweetened coconut milk, full fat
- 2 tsp. Thai yellow curry paste
- 3 tsp. soy sauce
- 1 tsp. honey
- 2 green onion chopped
- 4 cloves garlic, minced
- 2 Tbsp. fresh ginger, minced
- ¼ cup fresh cilantro, chopped
- ¼ cup spring onions, chopped

**Directions:**

1. Place coconut milk, curry paste, soy sauce and honey into a heavy stock pot.
2. Bring to a low simmer and cook until the spices are fragrant, about 30 minutes. Add water if necessary during cooking.
3. Transfer to serving bowls and garnish with cilantro and spring onions.
4. Serve hot.

**Nutrition Information Per Serving:**

- Total Fat: 29 grams
- Carbohydrates: 9 grams
- Protein: 14 grams

# Keto Red Curry

**Servings:** 6-8
**Time Required:** About 40 minutes
**Ingredients:**

- 1 cup broccoli florets
- 1 large handful fresh spinach
- 4 Tbsp. coconut oil
- ¼ medium onion
- 1 tsp. garlic, minced
- 1 tsp. fresh ginger, peeled and minced
- 2 tsp. soy sauce
- 1 Tbsp. red curry paste
- ½ cup coconut cream

**Directions:**

1. Add half the coconut oil to a sauce pan and heat over medium-high heat.
2. When the oil is hot, add the onion to the pan and saute for 3-4 minutes, until it is semi-translucent. Add the garlic to the pan and saute, stirring, just until fragrant, about 30 seconds.
3. Lower the heat to medium-low and add broccoli florets. Saute, stirring, for about 1-2 minutes.
4. Push the vegetables to the side of the pan and add the red curry paste. Saute until the paste is fragrant, then mix everything together.
5. Add the spinach on top of the vegetable mixture. When the spinach begins to wilt, add the coconut cream and stir.
6. Add the rest of the coconut oil, the soy sauce, and the minced ginger. Bring to a simmer for 5-10 minutes.
7. Serve hot.

**Nutrition Information Per Serving:**

- Total Fat: 41 grams
- Carbohydrates: 8 grams
- Protein: 4 grams

# *Kale Soup*

**Servings:** 6-8
**Time Required:** About 40 minutes
**Ingredients:**

- 4 cups fresh kale, chopped
- ½ cup canned white beans
- 2 cloves garlic, minced
- ½ onion, diced
- ½ cup celery, diced
- ¼ tsp. freshly ground black pepper
- Salt to taste
- 1 cup water

**Directions:**

1. Place all ingredients into a heavy stock pot.
2. Bring to a low simmer and cook until fragrant, about 30 minutes. Add water if necessary during cooking.
3. Transfer the soup to serving bowls and serve hot.

**Nutrition Information Per Serving**

- Total Fat: 15 grams
- Carbohydrates: 15 grams
- Protein: 9 grams

## *Creamy Jalapeno Soup*

**Servings:** 8-10
**Time Required:** About 45 minutes
**Ingredients:**

- 3 Tbsp. butter
- 2 cloves garlic, minced
- ½ onion, chopped
- ½ bell pepper, chopped
- 2 jalapeno peppers, seeded and chopped
- 6 oz. cream cheese
- 3 cups vegetable stock
- ½ cup heavy cream
- ¼ tsp. paprika
- 1 tsp. cumin
- 1 tsp. salt
- ½ tsp. freshly ground black pepper

**Directions:**

1. Heat the oil in a heavy stock pot over medium-high heat. When the butter is melted, add onion, bell pepper and jalapenos and sauté until the onion is soft, about 5 minutes.
2. Add the stock and cream cheese to the pot, stirring to combine.
3. Bring to a low simmer and cook until the chicken is thoroughly cooked and the vegetables are tender, about 30 minutes. Add water if necessary during cooking.
4. Stir in the cream, stirring to combine.
5. Transfer to serving bowls and serve hot topped with grated cheese.

**Nutrition Information Per Serving**

- Total Fat: 40 grams
- Carbohydrates: 4 grams
- Protein: 41 grams

# *Chinese Chili Soup*

**Servings:** 8-10
**Time Required:** About 40 minutes
**Ingredients:**

- ¼ cup sesame oil
- 6 dried red Thai chilis
- 5 cloves garlic, crushed
- 2 Tbsp. fresh ginger, peeled and sliced
- 3 cups vegetable stock
- ¼ cup soy sauce
- ¼ cup dry sherry
- Salt to taste
- ¼ cup fresh Thai basil, chopped

**Directions:**

1. Heat the oil in a heavy stock pot over medium-high heat. Add the garlic, chilis and ginger to the pot and sauté just until fragrant, about a minute.
2. Lower the heat and add all the other ingredients, excluding the basil, to the pot.
3. Bring to a low simmer and cook until the soup is fragrant, about 30 minutes. Add water if necessary during cooking.
4. Bring the soup to a boil again and stir in the basil, stirring until the basil is fragrant and wilted.
5. Transfer to serving bowls and serve hot.

**Nutrition Information Per Serving:**

- Total Fat: 15 grams
- Carbohydrates: 7 grams
- Protein: 31 grams

## *Mushroom Soup*

**Servings:** 8-10

**Time Required:** About 40 minutes

**Ingredients:**

- 1 onion, chopped
- 3 cloves garlic, minced
- 2 cups fresh button mushrooms, chopped
- 1 medium yellow summer squash, chopped
- 3 cups vegetable stock
- Salt and pepper to taste
- 1 tsp. poultry seasoning

**Directions:**

1. Add all ingredients to a heavy stock pot.
2. Bring to a low simmer and cook until the soup is fragrant, about 30 minutes. Add water if necessary during cooking.
3. Transfer soup to serving bowls and serve hot.

**Nutrition Information Per Serving**

- Total Fat: 15 grams
- Carbohydrates: 9 grams
- Protein: 30 grams

# *Vietnamese-Style Vegetable Soup*

**Servings:** 6-8
**Time Required:** About 40 minutes
**Ingredients:**

- 1 onion, diced
- 2 Tbsp. tomato paste
- 2 whole star anise
- 1 Tbsp. fresh ginger, peeled and minced
- 3 cloves garlic, minced
- 6 cups water
- 1 tsp. ground pepper
- ½ tsp. Chinese five-spice
- ½ tsp. curry powder
- 2 carrots, peeled and sliced

**Directions:**

1. Place all ingredients in a heavy stock pot.
2. Bring to a low simmer and cook until the soup is fragrant, about 30 minutes. Add water if necessary during cooking.
3. Serve the stew hot.

**Nutrition Information Per Serving**

- Total Fat: 9 grams
- Carbohydrates: 8 grams
- Protein: 15 grams

# *Green Chili Soup*

**Servings:** 6-8
**Time Required:** About 2 hours
**Ingredients:**

- ½ cup dry navy beans, soaked for an hour in hot water
- 1 onion diced
- 3 New Mexico green chili peppers, chopped
- 5 cloves garlic, minced
- 1 cup cauliflower, diced
- 4 cups vegetable stock
- ¼ cup fresh cilantro, chopped
- 1 tsp. ground coriander
- 1 tsp. ground cumin
- 1 tsp. salt
- 2 oz. cream cheese

**Directions:**

1. Put all the ingredients, excluding the cream cheese, into a large heavy stock pot.
2. Bring to a low simmer and cook until the beans are tender, about 60 minutes. Add water if necessary during cooking.
3. Using an immersion blender, blend the soup until it is smooth.
4. Return the soup to a simmer.
5. When the soup is bubbly, stir in the cream cheese until it's melted.
6. Transfer the soup to serving bowls and serve hot.

**Nutrition Information Per Serving:**

- Total Fat: 5 grams
- Carbohydrates: 13 grams
- Protein: 22 grams

# *Vegetarian Red Chili*

**Servings:** 6-8
**Time Required:** About 35 minutes
**Ingredients:**

- 3 tsp. chili powder
- 2 tsp. ground cumin
- 2 tsp. salt
- 1 tsp. dried oregano
- 1 Tbsp. olive oil
- 1 onion, chopped
- 2 cloves garlic, minced
- 1 cup canned diced tomatoes
- 1 Tbsp. canned chipotle chilis, chopped
- 2 corn tortillas, torn into small pieces
- ½ cup water

**Directions:**

1. In a small bowl, mix chili powder, cumin, salt and oregano.
2. In a blender or food processor, blend tomatoes, chilis, and tortilla pieces until smooth.
3. Heat the oil in a heavy stock pot over medium-high heat. When the oil is hot, sauté the onions until they're softened, about 3 minutes. Add the garlic and sauté for about a minute more.
4. Stir in the spice mixture and sauté until fragrant, about 30 seconds.
5. Add the tomato/tortilla mixture to the pot, along with 2 cups water.
6. Bring to a low simmer and cook until fragrant about 20 minutes. Add water if necessary during cooking.
7. Transfer the chili to serving bowls and serve hot.

**Nutrition Information Per Serving**

- Total Fat: 24 grams
- Carbohydrates: 12 grams
- Protein: 30 grams

## *Vegetarian Green Chili*

**Servings:** 6-8
**Time Required:** About 30 minutes
**Ingredients:**

- 3 tomatillos, sliced
- 3 jalapeno peppers, seeded and chopped
- 2 New Mexico green chili peppers, seeded and chopped
- 6 cloves garlic, minced
- 1 tomato, chopped
- 3 cups vegetable stock
- 2 tsp. cumin
- Salt and pepper to taste

**Directions:**

1. Put the tomatillos, jalapenos, New Mexico chilis, garlic, chicken stock and tomato into a heavy stock pot.
2. Add the cumin, salt, and pepper on top of the meat.
3. Bring to a low simmer and cook until fragrant, about 20 minutes. Add water if necessary during cooking.
4. Using an immersion blender, blend the sauce in the pot until it's smooth.
5. Transfer the chili to serving bowls and serve hot, garnished with chopped fresh cilantro.

**Nutrition Information Per Serving:**

- Total Fat: 4 grams
- Carbohydrates: 4 grams
- Protein: 26 grams

# *Tortilla Soup*

**Servings:** 6-8
**Time Required:** About 30 minutes
**Ingredients:**

- 2 corn tortillas, torn into pieces
- ½ onion, chopped
- 1 cup tomatoes, chopped
- 2 cloves garlic
- 1 Tbsp. canned chipotle chili in adobo sauce, chopped
- ½ jalapeno pepper
- ¼ cup fresh cilantro, chopped
- 1 tsp. salt
- 1 Tbsp. olive oil
- 4 cups water

**Directions:**

1. In a blender or food processor, combine onion, tomatoes, garlic, chipotle, jalapeno and cilantro. Blend until the mixture is smooth.
2. Heat the oil in a heavy stock pot over medium-high heat. When the oil is hot, add the blended mixture to the pot. Cook, stirring, until fragrant, about a minute or two.
3. Add the tortillas, chicken, and water to the pot.
4. Bring to a low simmer and cook until fragrant, about 20 minutes. Add water if necessary during cooking.
5. Transfer to serving bowls and serve hot.

**Nutrition Information Per Serving:**

- Total Fat: 5 grams
- Carbohydrates: 5 grams
- Protein: 12 grams

## *Keto Vegetable Soup*

**Servings:** 6-8
**Time Required:** About 45 minutes
**Ingredients:**

- 1 turnip, cut into bite-size pieces
- 1 onion, chopped
- 6 stalks celery, diced
- 1 carrot, sliced
- 15 oz. pumpkin puree
- 1 lb. green beans frozen or fresh
- 8 cups chicken stock
- 2 cups water
- 1 Tbsp. fresh basil, chopped
- ¼ tsp. thyme leaves
- 1/8 tsp. rubbed sage
- Salt to taste
- 1 lb. fresh spinach, chopped

**Directions:**

1. Put all the ingredients, excluding the spinach, into a heavy stock pot.
2. Bring to a low simmer and cook until the vegetables are tender, about 30 minutes. Add water if necessary during cooking.
3. Add the spinach and stir until it's wilted, about 5 minutes.
4. Transfer to serving bowls and serve hot.

**Nutrition Information Per Serving:**

- Total Fat: 0 gram
- Carbohydrates: 10 grams
- Protein: 3 grams

# *Keto Cabbage Soup*

**Servings:** 6-8
**Time Required:** About 45 minutes
**Ingredients:**

- ¼ cup onion, diced
- 1 clove garlic, minced
- 1 tsp. cumin
- 1 head cabbage, chopped
- 1 ¼ cup canned diced tomatoes
- 5 oz. canned green chilis
- 4 cups vegetable stock
- Salt and pepper to taste

**Directions:**

1. Heat a heavy stock pot over medium-high heat. When the oil is hot, add the onions and sauté for 5-7 minutes more. Add the garlic and sauté for one more minute.
2. Bring to a low simmer and cook until the vegetables are tender, about 30 minutes. Add water if necessary during cooking.
3. Transfer to serving bowls and serve hot.

**Nutrition Information Per Serving:**

- Total Fat: 18 grams
- Carbohydrates: 6 grams
- Protein: 17 grams

# Lunch

Meat, poultry and fish are a big part of most keto diets, but it's possible to prepare vegetarian dishes that fit well within the requirements of a keto-friendly nutrition plan. The recipes in this section include main dishes, vegetable side dishes and desserts, all of them vegetarian and some them vegan-friendly, as well. For our lunch recipes, we've concentrated on dishes that are light enough (and easy enough to prepare) that they'll fit perfectly into your mid-day routine. They aren't deficient in flavor, though, and they're interesting enough to be a hearty part of dinner, if you decide to prepare them a little later in the day.

# *Asian Cabbage Salad*

**Servings:** 6-8
**Time Required:** About 45 minutes (plus marinating time)
**Ingredients:**

- 15 oz. extra firm tofu
- 1 Tbsp. soy sauce
- 1 Tbsp. sesame oil
- 1 Tbsp. water
- 2 tsp. minced garlic
- 1 Tbsp. rice wine vinegar
- Juice of ½ lemon
- 9 oz. bok choy
- 1 green onion
- 2 Tbsp. fresh cilantro, chopped
- 3 Tbsp. coconut oil
- 2 Tbsp. soy sauce
- 1 Tbsp. peanut butter
- Juice of ½ lime
- ½ tsp. sugar-free sweetener

**Directions:**

1. Wrap the tofu in a clean kitchen towel and put something heavy over the top. Allow the tofu to sit for 4-6 hours; this will press the moisture out of the tofu, and you may need to replace the towel with a dry one mid-way through the process.
2. Combine the soy sauce, sesame oil, water, garlic, vinegar, and lemon in a medium bowl.
3. Cut the tofu into 1-inch squares and place into a large zip-close plastic bag. Add the marinade to the bag and marinate in the refrigerator for at least a half hour (overnight is better).
4. At the end of the marinating time, pre-heat the oven to 350 degrees Fahrenheit.
5. Arrange the tofu squares on a parchment-lined baking sheet. Put the sheet on the oven's center rack and bake for 30-35 minutes.
6. In the meantime, chop the cilantro and the green onion.

7. Mix together the rest of the ingredients, excluding the lime juice and the bok choy, in a medium bowl. Toss in the cilantro and onion.
8. Once the tofu is almost cooked, add lime juice into the salad dressing and mix together.
9. Chop the bok choy into bite-size pieces.
10. Remove the tofu from the oven and toss together with the other ingredients.

**Nutrition Information Per Serving:**

- Total Fat: 31 grams
- Carbohydrates: 7 grams
- Protein: 24 grams

## *Spicy Mushrooms*

**Servings:** 2
**Time Required:** About 20 minutes
**Ingredients:**

- 8 oz. white mushrooms, chopped
- 2 large chili peppers, such as guajillo, poblano or New Mexico, seeded and chopped
- 1 tsp. olive oil
- 1 onion, chopped
- 6 cloves garlic, minced
- 1 tsp. ground cumin
- ½ tsp. dried oregano
- ½ tsp. smoked paprika
- ¼ tsp. ground cinnamon
- ¼ tsp. salt
- ¼ cup water
- 1 tsp. cider vinegar

**Directions:**

1. Heat the oil in a large skillet over medium-high heat. When the oil is hot, add the onions to the pan and sauté until soft and translucent, about 5 minutes.
2. Add garlic to the pan and sauté for one minute more.
3. Transfer half of the onion and garlic to a blender or food processor.
4. Add mushrooms to the skillet and cook for 5 minutes more.
5. Meanwhile, add chilis to the blender or food processor. Add cumin, oregano, paprika, cinnamon, salt and water. Blend until smooth.
6. Transfer the blended sauce mixture to the skillet.
7. Simmer until the sauce is heated through and bubbly, about 5 minutes.
8. Serve the mushrooms hot with steamed cauliflower.

**Nutrition Information Per Serving:**

- Total Fat: 12 grams
- Carbohydrates: 16 grams
- Protein: 4 grams

# *Herby Zucchini Noodles*

**Servings:** 2
**Time Required:** About 20 minutes
**Ingredients:**

- 3 medium zucchini
- ½ tsp. salt
- ½ avocado
- 1 cup fresh basil leaves
- ¼ cup walnuts
- 2 cloves garlic
- ½ lemon
- ¼ cup Parmesan cheese, grated
- 1 Tbsp. olive oil
- Salt and pepper to taste

**Directions:**

1. Using a vegetable peeler, cut the zucchini into very thin ribbons. Use only the skin and outer flesh of the zucchini, stopping once you reach the seeds in the center.
2. Toss the zucchini with salt in a colander. Set aside.
3. Place avocado, basil, walnuts, garlic, lemon, and cheese in blender or food processor and pulse until smooth. Add water to adjust the consistency if necessary.
4. Heat 1 tablespoon olive oil in a skillet over medium heat.
5. Saute zucchini until it begins to soften, about 3-5 minutes. Transfer to a mixing bowl.
6. Gently toss the zucchini with the dressing until well coated.

**Nutrition Information Per Serving:**

- Total Fat: 27 grams
- Carbohydrates: 11 grams
- Protein: 11 grams

## *Keto Deviled Eggs*

**Servings:** 4
**Time Required:** 15 minutes
**Ingredients:**

- 8 eggs
- ¼ cup mayonnaise
- 2 tsp. mustard
- 1 tsp. lemon juice
- 1 tsp. smoked paprika
- Salt and pepper

**Directions:**

1. Hard boil the eggs, peel and then slice in half lengthwise.
2. Slice in half lengthwise.
3. Carefully remove the egg yolks from the whites. In a medium bowl, use a fork to mash the yolks with mayonnaise, mustard, vinegar, salt and pepper to taste.
4. Carefully spoon the yolk mixture back into the hollows in the egg whited.
5. Sprinkle with smoked paprika.

**Nutrition Information Per Serving:**

- Total Fat: 20 grams
- Carbohydrates: 0 grams
- Protein: 12 grams

## *Cheesy Cauliflower Nuggets*

**Servings:** 4
**Time Required:** About 25 minutes
**Ingredients:**

- 1 medium cauliflower, riced
- 1 ½ cups cheddar cheese, shredded
- 3 eggs
- 2 tsp. paprika
- 1 tsp. turmeric
- ¾ tsp. rosemary

**Directions:**

1. If you're starting with a whole head of cauliflower, carefully core it and chop it into florets. Place the florets into a food processor and pulse until the cauliflower is the consistency of grains of rice. Alternatively, you can purchase pre-riced cauliflower.
2. Place cauliflower into a microwave safe bowl, and microwave for 5-7 minutes.
3. Carefully place the cauliflower on a double layer of paper towel and cover with another double layer. Press firmly on the cauliflower to extract as much moisture from it as you can.
4. Transfer the pressed cauliflower to a medium mixing bowl. Add eggs one at a time, and then add the cheese.
5. Add the seasoning ingredients and then mix everything thoroughly with a wooden spoon or your hands.
6. Heat the oils in a skillet over medium-high heat.
7. Form the cauliflower into 1-inch balls and then flatten them slight in your palm.
8. Place the cauliflower nuggets into the hot oil and fry until they're crispy on the bottom, about 2 minutes. Flip them and fry until the other side is crispy.
9. Serve hot.

**Nutrition Information Per Serving:**

- Total Fat: 3 grams
- Carbohydrates: 1 gram
- Protein: 3 grams

# Keto Egg Salad

**Servings:** 8-10
**Time Required:** About 25 minutes
**Ingredients:**

- 10 eggs
- 2 Tbsp. mayonnaise
- 1 tsp. Dijon mustard
- ¼ tsp. smoked paprika
- 1 spring onion, diced
- Salt and pepper to taste

**Directions:**

1. Place the eggs in a large pot covered with an inch of cold water. Bring the water to a boil and boil the eggs for 8-10 minutes. Remove them and cool them quickly in cold water.
2. Shell the eggs and transfer them to a cutting board. Chop the eggs coarsely and transfer to a mixing bowl.
3. Add the rest of the ingredients to the mixing bowl toss well to combine.
4. Serve garnished with chopped chives.

**Nutrition Information Per Serving:**

- Total Fat: 26 grams
- Carbohydrates: 2 grams
- Protein: 16 grams

## *Cheesy Vegetable Dip*

**Servings:** 6
**Time Required:** About 35 minutes
**Ingredients:**

- 1 can (14 oz.) hearts of palm, drained
- 3 green onions, chopped
- ¼ cup mayonnaise
- 2 Tbsp. Italian seasoning
- ½ cup Parmesan cheese, grated
- 2 large eggs

**Directions:**

1. Pre-heat oven to 350 degrees Fahrenheit.
2. Lightly coat a small baking dish with cooking oil spray
3. Add all the ingredients, excluding the eggs, to a food processor and pulse until the mixture is well-combined but still slightly chunky.
4. Add the eggs and pulse again briefly, just enough to combine.
5. Spoon the dip into the baking dish and bake for 15-20 minutes, until the dip is starting to bubble.
6. Carefully stir the dip and sprinkle the top with a bit more Parmesan cheese.
7. Return to the oven and bake until the top is beginning to brown, about 10 minutes.

**Nutrition Information Per Serving:**

- Total Fat: 9 grams
- Carbohydrates: 3 grams
- Protein: 5 grams

# Keto Hummus

**Servings:** 6
**Time Required:** About 20 minutes
**Ingredients:**

- 3 cups cauliflower florets
- 2 Tbsp. water
- 2 Tbsp. olive oil
- ½ tsp. salt
- 3 cloves garlic
- 1 ½ Tbsp. tahini paste
- 3 Tbsp. fresh lemon juice
- 3 additional Tbsp. olive oil
- ¾ tsp. kosher salt

**Directions:**

1. Add the cauliflower, water, olive oil, salt, and garlic cloves to a microwave safe dish. Microwave for about 15 minutes until cauliflower is soft.
2. Transfer the mixture to a blender or food processor and blend until it's smooth. Add the tahini, lemon juice, additional olive oil, and kosher salt. Blend until smooth.

**Nutrition Information Per Serving:**

- Total Fat: 14 grams
- Carbohydrates: 4 grams
- Protein: 2 grams

# Mexican-Style Dip

**Servings:** 16
**Time Required:** About 35 minutes
**Ingredients:**

- 4 cups cauliflower florets, cooked and drained
- 2 Tbsp. mayonnaise
- 1 tsp. Cajun seasoning
- 3 Tbsp. heavy whipping cream
- ½ tsp. ground cumin
- 3 Tbsp. canned chipotle
- 1 Tbsp. olive oil
- 2 cups avocado, mashed
- 2 tsp. fresh lime juice
- ½ tsp. kosher salt
- ¼ tsp. ground black pepper
- 2 cups sour cream
- 1 cup tomatoes, chopped
- 1 cup cheddar cheese, shredded
- ½ cup scallions, chopped
- ¼ cup black olives, sliced

**Directions:**

1. Combine the cooked cauliflower, mayonnaise, Cajun seasoning, heavy whipping cream, cumin, chipotle, and oil in a blender or food processor.
2. Blend until smooth.
3. Mash the avocados with a fork, leaving them slightly chunky
4. Stir in the lime juice, salt and pepper.
5. Spread the cauliflower layer evenly over the bottom of a casserole dish.
6. Spread the sour cream over the cauliflower.
7. Spoon the avocado on top of the sour cream and gently spread it out to form a layer on top of the sour cream.
8. Sprinkle the chopped tomatoes over the avocado.
9. Spread the shredded cheese over the tomatoes, followed by the scallions.
10. Finally, evenly sprinkle the olives on top.
11. Can be stored in the refrigerator for up to five days.

**Nutrition Information Per Serving:**

- Total Fat: 15 grams
- Carbohydrates: 6 grams
- Protein: 4 grams

## *Keto Cobb Salad*

**Servings:** 2
**Time Required:** About 10 minutes
**Ingredients:**

- 2 Tbsp. sour cream
- 2 Tbsp. mayonnaise
- ½ tsp. garlic powder
- ½ tsp. onion powder
- 1 tsp. dried parsley
- 1 Tbsp. milk
- 3 eggs, hard boiled and sliced
- 4 oz. cheddar cheese, shredded
- 3 cups romaine lettuce, torn into bite-size chunks
- ½ cup cherry tomatoes, cut in half
- 1 cup cucumber, diced

**Directions:**

1. In a small bowl, stir together the sour cream, mayonnaise, and herbs until combined.
2. Stir in the milk to complete the dressing.
3. Assemble the vegetables, egg and cheese on serving plates.
4. Spoon the dressing, about 2 tablespoons per serving, on top of the salad and toss gently to coat.

**Nutrition Information Per Serving:**

- Total Fat: 26 grams
- Carbohydrates: 5 grams
- Protein: 17 grams

## *Zesty Broccoli Slaw*

**Servings:** 4
**Time Required:** About 10 minutes
**Ingredients:**

- 12 oz. bag broccoli slaw
- 2 Tbsp. olive oil
- 1 Tbsp. coconut aminos
- 1 tsp. fresh ginger, grated
- ½ tsp. salt
- ¼ tsp. pepper
- ½ cup full fat plain yogurt
- ½ Tbsp. sesame seeds

**Directions:**

1. Heat the olive oil in a large skillet over medium-high heat. Stir in the broccoli slaw and then cover the skillet, lower the heat to medium, and cook for 5-7 minutes.
2. Uncover and stir the rest of the ingredients, excluding the yogurt and sesame seeds.
3. Remove the pan from the heat and add the yogurt.
4. Transfer to serving plates and sprinkle with sesame seeds.
5. Uncover, then stir in the coconut aminos, ginger, salt and pepper. Remove your skillet from the heat, then add yogurt and top with sesame seeds.

**Nutrition Information Per Serving:**

- Total Fat: 5 grams
- Carbohydrates: 4 grams
- Protein: 2 grams

# *Pan-Roasted Vegetable Salad*

**Servings:** 2
**Time Required:** About 10 minutes
**Ingredients:**

- 2 Tbsp. poppy seeds
- 2 Tbsp. sesame seeds
- 1 tsp. onion flakes
- 1 tsp. garlic powder
- 4 oz. goat cheese, sliced ½-inch thick
- 1 medium red bell pepper, seeded and sliced
- ½ cup baby portobello mushrooms, sliced
- 4 cups arugula
- 1 Tbsp. olive oil

**Directions:**

1. Combine the poppy and sesame seeds, onion, and garlic powder in a small bowl.
2. Dredge the cheese slices in the mixture to coat both sides, then set aside on a plate in the refrigerator.
3. Heat a skillet sprayed with cooking oil over medium heat. Place the peppers and mushrooms in the pan and cook, without stir, just until they begin to brown and soften.
4. Meanwhile, divide the arugula between two serving plates.
5. Layer the peppers and mushrooms on top of the arugula.
6. Take the cheese from the refrigerator and lightly sauté for about 30 seconds on each side, just until it begins to soften.
7. Top the salad with the cheese slices and drizzle with olive oil.

**Nutrition Information Per Serving:**

- Total Fat: 28 grams
- Carbohydrates: 7 grams
- Protein: 16 grams

## *Mediterranean Garden Wraps*

**Servings:** 4
**Time Required:** About 10 minutes
**Ingredients:**

- 1 cup full fat plain yogurt
- 1 tsp. garlic powder
- 1 Tbsp. white vinegar
- 2 Tbsp. olive oil
- ¼ cucumber, peeled, seeded and grated
- 2 Tbsp. minced fresh dill
- Salt and pepper to taste
- 4 large collard green leaves
- 1 medium cucumber, julienned
- ½ medium red bell pepper, seeded and sliced
- ½ cup purple onion, diced
- 8 kalamata olives, sliced
- 4 oz. feta cheese, cut into 4 strips
- 4 large cherry tomatoes, halved

**Directions:**

1. Whisk the first seven ingredients together in a medium mixing bowl and set aside in the refrigerator.
2. Wash the collard greens and remove the tough stem.
3. Evenly spread two tablespoons of the sauce mixture across the center of each leaf.
4. Place the vegetables and feta in the center of the leaves, dividing equally between the two leaves.
5. Fold the top and bottom of the leaves over the filling in the center, then roll the leaves from one side to the other like a burrito.
6. Serve with more sauce for dipping.

**Nutrition Information Per Serving:**

- Total Fat: 11 grams
- Carbohydrates: 7 grams
- Protein: 7 grams

## *Mini Mozzarella Pie*

**Servings:** 4
**Time Required:** About 40 minutes
**Ingredients:**

- 1 cup almond flour
- 1 large egg
- 3 Tbsp. mozzarella whey
- 1 tsp. garlic powder
- ¼ cup Parmesan cheese, grated
- 2 Tbsp. prepared pesto
- 3-4 leaves fresh basil
- ½ oz. fresh mozzarella cheese (with whey)
- 3-4 cherry tomatoes

**Directions:**

1. Pre-heat oven to 375 degrees Fahrenheit. and line a cookie sheet with parchment. Spray with non stick spray.
2. Combine the almond flour, garlic powder, and mozzarella whey in a bowl.
3. Add the egg and Parmesan cheese then mix with a wooden spoon to make dough.
4. Form the dough into a ball and place on a parchment-lined baking sheet that's been lightly sprayed with cooking spray.
5. Using wet fingers, press the dough ball into a circle ½-inch thick.
6. Spread pesto evenly in the center of the dough. Place the mozzarella, basil leaves, and tomatoes in layers in the center of the dough.
7. Carefully fold the edges of the dough toward the center, working around the circle until the dough is completely folded over.
8. Put the sheet onto the oven's center rack and bake until the dough is beginning to brown, about 20-25 minutes.
9. Serve hot.

**Nutrition Information Per Serving:**

- Total Fat: 24 grams
- Carbohydrates: 8 grams
- Protein: 14 grams

## Mushroom Cauliflower Bowls

**Servings:** 4
**Time Required:** About 40 minutes
**Ingredients:**

- 6 oz. baby portobello mushrooms, sliced
- 3 cloves garlic, minced
- 1 Tbsp. rosemary
- ½ cup walnuts, chopped
- 1 Tbsp. smoked paprika
- 2 Tbsp. olive oil
- 1 medium head cauliflower
- ½ cup water
- 1 cup half and half
- 1 cup sharp cheddar cheese, shredded
- 2 Tbsp. butter
- Salt to taste

**Directions:**

1. Pre-heat oven to 400 degrees Fahrenheit.
2. In a small mixing bowl, combine mushrooms, garlic, rosemary, walnuts, paprika and olive oil. Toss everything to coat well.
3. Spread the mixture on a foil-lined baking sheet. Place in the oven and bake for 15 minutes.
4. Core and chop the cauliflower. Place it in a food processor and pulse until its texture is fine.
5. Place the ground cauliflower in a medium sauce pan with ½ cup water and bring to a boil. Cover, lower the heat and steam for five minutes.
6. Uncover and pour in the half and half. Stir and allow to simmer for 3 minutes.
7. Lower the heat to low and stir in the cheese. Stir until the cheese is melted and creamy. Season to taste with salt.
8. Transfer the cauliflower to serving bowls and top with hot mushroom mixture.

**Nutrition Information Per Serving:**

- Total Fat: 37 grams
- Carbohydrates: 11 grams
- Protein: 15 grams

# Dinner

For the main meal of the day, you're going to want something as substantial as it is delicious. These recipes fit that bill. We've brought together an irresistible collection of main dishes, sides, and appetizers that can work together in combination to make a keto-vegetarian feast or own their own for a quick weeknight dinner. The focus here is on complete nutrition, all within the framework of both the keto and vegetarian diets, that doesn't sacrifice any flavor.

## *Palak Paneer*

**Servings:** 4
**Time Required:** About 10 minutes
**Ingredients:**

- 1 lb. fresh spinach
- 1 ½ cups paneer
- 2 tsp. olive oil
- 5 cloves garlic, minced
- 1 Tbsp. fresh ginger, peeled and minced
- 1 onion, chopped
- 2 tomatoes, chopped
- 2 tsp. ground cumin
- ½ tsp. cayenne pepper
- 2 tsp. garam masala
- 1 tsp. turmeric
- 1 tsp. salt
- ½ cup water

**Directions:**

1. Heat the oil in a large, heavy skillet over medium-high heat. When the oil is hot, add the garlic and ginger and sauté just until fragrant, about 30 seconds.
2. Add the rest of the ingredients, excluding the paneer, and stir to combine.
3. Sautee until the spinach is wilted and the spices are fragrant, about 4-5 minutes.
4. Carefully add the paneer to the pot, stirring gently to combine.
5. Serve hot.

**Nutrition Information Per Serving:**

- Total Fat: 16 grams
- Carbohydrates: 8 grams
- Protein: 11 grams

# *Cauliflower Curry*

**Servings:** 4-6
**Time Required:** About 30 minutes
**Ingredients:**

- 1 head cauliflower, chopped
- ½ onion, chopped
- 2 tomatoes, chopped
- 6 cloves garlic, minced
- 1 Tbsp. fresh ginger, peeled and minced
- ½ jalapeno chili, diced
- 1 tsp. olive oil
- ½ tsp. turmeric
- 1 tsp. ground cumin
- ½ tsp. garam masala
- ¾ tsp. salt
- ½ tsp. paprika

**Directions:**

1. Place onion, tomato, chili, ginger and garlic in a blender or food processor and blend until smooth.
2. Heat the oil in a large skillet over medium-high heat. When the oil is hot, add mixture from the blender to the pan.
3. Add the spices to the pan and stir to mix. Simmer for 5 minutes.
4. Stir the cauliflower into the pan and simmer until tender, about 15 minutes.
5. Serve hot.

**Nutrition Information Per Serving:**

- Total Fat: 1 gram
- Carbohydrates: 20 grams
- Protein: 4 grams

## Green Chili Cheese Bake

**Servings:** 4
**Time Required:** About 35 minutes
**Ingredients:**

- 4 eggs, beaten
- 1 cup half and half
- 10 oz. canned green chilis
- ½ tsp. salt
- ½ tsp. ground cumin
- 1 cup Monterey Jack cheese, grated
- ¼ cup fresh cilantro, chopped

**Directions:**

1. Preheat oven to 350 degrees Fahrenheit.
2. In a medium bowl, combine eggs, half and half, chilis, cheese, salt and cumin.
3. Pour the mixture into a greased baking pan. Cover the pan with aluminum foil.
4. Place the pan on the oven's center rack and bake until the egg is set, about 25-30 minutes.
5. Remove the pan from the pot and allow to cool slightly before serving.

**Nutrition Information Per Serving:**

- Total Fat: 19 grams
- Carbohydrates: 6 grams
- Protein: 14 grams

# *Indian-Style Eggplant*

**Servings:** 4
**Time Required:** About 30 minutes
**Ingredients:**

- 1 medium eggplant, peeled and sliced
- 1/3 cup olive oil
- 3 cloves garlic, minced
- ½ onion, chopped
- ¼ tsp. turmeric
- 1/8 tsp. cayenne pepper
- ½ tsp. salt
- 1/3 cup tomatoes, diced
- ½ cup water
- 2 Tbsp. fresh cilantro, chopped

**Directions:**

1. Heat 2 tablespoons of the olive oil in a large, heavy skillet. Once the oil is hot, add enough eggplant slices to cover the bottom of the pot liner. Allow the eggplant to brown well on the bottom, and add more eggplant as the slices shrink. Add more oil as necessary.
2. When the eggplant is browned and softened, add the onions and sauté for 5 minutes more.
3. Add the garlic and sauté for another minute.
4. Add the turmeric, cayenne, and salt. Sauté until fragrant, about a minute.
5. Add the tomatoes and water, and stir to combine everything in the pan.
6. Bring to a simmer and cook until the eggplant is fully cooked, about 15 minutes.
7. Transfer the eggplant and sauce to a serving platter.
8. Serve hot, garnished with cilantro.

**Nutrition Information Per Serving:**

- Total Fat: 12 grams
- Carbohydrates: 6 grams
- Protein: 1 gram

## Keto Pizza

**Servings:** 4
**Time Required:** About 30 minutes
**Ingredients:**

- 6 oz. mozzarella cheese
- ½ cup almond flour
- 2 Tbsp. psyllium husk
- 2 Tbsp. cream cheese
- 2 Tbsp. Parmesan cheese
- 1 large egg
- 1 tsp. Italian seasoning
- ½ tsp. salt
- ½ tsp. pepper
- 4 oz. cheddar cheese, shredded
- 1 medium vine tomato
- ¼ cup sugar-free marinara Sauce
- 2/3 medium bell pepper
- 2 Tbsp. fresh basil, chopped

**Directions:**

1. Preheat oven to 400 degrees Fahrenheit.
2. Combine almond flour, psyllium husk, parmesan cheese, Italian seasoning, salt, and pepper in a large mixing bowl.
3. Put mozzarella cheese is a microwave-safe bowl and microwave about 1 minute until it is soft. Remove from microwave and place cream cheese on top of the mozzarella in the bowl.
4. Stir egg into the dry ingredients in the mixing bowl. Add the heated cheeses to the bowl and mix thoroughly to create a dough.
5. Divide the dough into two equal portions and roll them out into a ¼-inch-thick crust on a lightly greased baking sheet.
6. Put the baking sheet into the oven and bake until the dough is just beginning to brown, about 10 minutes.
7. Remove the crust from the oven and allow to cool slightly.
8. Spread 2 tablespoons of marinara sauce on each pizza and top with 2 ounces cheddar cheese and chopped bell pepper.
9. Return the pizzas to the oven and bake for another 8-10 minutes.
10. Remove from the oven and serve hot.

**Nutrition Information Per Serving:**

- Total Fat: 31 grams
- Carbohydrates: 6 grams
- Protein: 23 grams

## *Spaghetti Squash*

**Servings:** 4

**Time Required:** About 60 minutes

**Ingredients:**

- 1 spaghetti squash, medium

**Directions:**

1. Preheat oven to 400 degrees Fahrenheit.
2. With a sharp knife, carefully cut the squash in half crosswise, across the short length of the squash instead of along the longer axis.
3. Place the squash halves on a baking sheet, cut side down.
4. Place the baking sheet on the oven's center rack and roast until the squash is tender, about 45-50 minutes.
5. Remove the squash and, while it's still hot, carefully shred the flesh into spaghetti-like strands with a fork.
6. Serve the squash hot with butter.

**Nutrition Information Per Serving:**

- Total Fat: 1 gram
- Carbohydrates: 7 grams
- Protein: 1 gram

## Steamed Artichokes

**Servings:** 4
**Time Required:** About 40 minutes
**Ingredients:**

- 4 artichokes, medium-sized
- 1 lemon
- 4 cups vegetable stock
- ¼ tsp. kosher salt

**Directions:**

1. Trim the artichoke stems to an inch in length. Trim the other end of the artichokes, too, cutting the inch from the ends of the leaves. Discard the trimmings.
2. Slice the lemon into four slices.
3. Place the steamer rack into the steamer pot and place the lemon slices on the rack. Place the artichokes, stem end up, on the lemon slices, one artichoke on each lemon slice.
4. Pour the stock carefully into the pot. Season with salt.
5. Cover the pot.
6. Steam until the artichokes are tender, about 25-35 minutes.
7. Serve the artichokes with melted butter for dipping.

**Nutrition Information Per Serving:**

- Total Fat: 1 gram
- Carbohydrates: 13 grams
- Protein: 4 grams

## *Cheesy Cauliflower Casserole*

**Servings:** 4-6
**Time Required:** About 60 minutes
**Ingredients:**

- 1 head cauliflower
- 2 eggs
- 2 Tbsp. heavy cream
- 2 oz. cream cheese
- ½ cup sour cream
- ½ cup Parmesan cheese, grated
- 1 cup cheddar cheese, grated
- 2 Tbsp. butter
- 1 cup water

**Directions:**

1. Preheat oven to 350 degrees Fahrenheit.
2. Add eggs, cream, sour cream, cream cheese, parmesan and cheddar cheese to a blender or food processor. Blend to combine.
3. Add cauliflower to the food processor and blend, pulsing so that you can stop when the mixture is still chunky, not smooth.
4. Grease a casserole pan and pour the mixture into the pan.
5. Place the pan on the oven's center rack and bake until the casserole is bubbly, about 45 minutes.
6. Remove the pan and serve the casserole hot.

**Nutrition Information Per Serving:**

- Total Fat: 28 grams
- Carbohydrates: 7 grams
- Protein: 17 grams

# Thai-Style Zucchini Noodles

**Servings:** 3
**Time Required:** About 25 minutes
**Ingredients:**

- 2 medium zucchini, spiralized
- ½ cup sliced mushrooms
- 1 cup shredded broccoli slaw mix
- 1 tsp. sesame oil
- ¼ cup almond butter
- 2 Tbsp. soy sauce
- 2 Tbsp. sesame oil
- ¼ tsp. garlic powder
- 1 tsp. crushed red pepper flakes
- 1 tsp. sugar-free sweetener

**Directions:**

1. Heat sesame oil in a large skillet on medium heat. Add the shredded broccoli slaw mix and mushrooms, sautéing until the vegetables have softened.
2. Cut zucchini noodles using a vegetable spiralizer or a vegetable peeler. Press the noodles between paper towels to remove some of their moisture.
3. Heat the noodles in the skillet, stirring often, until they're soft but not mushy, about 3-5 minutes.
4. Combine the rest of the ingredients in a small mixing bowl and whisk together. Adjust the consistency with water if necessary to make a sauce.
5. Divide the noodles evenly between three serving bowls and top with the sauce.

**Nutrition Information Per Serving:**

- Total Fat: 24 grams
- Carbohydrates: 6 grams
- Protein: 8 grams

# *Keto Italian-Style Dumplings*

**Servings:** 5
**Time Required:** About 30 minutes
**Ingredients:**
*For dough:*

- 2 cups almond flour
- 2 cups mozzarella cheese, shredded
- ¼ cup butter
- 1 large egg
- 1 large egg yolk

*For sauce:*

- ¼ cup salted butter
- 1 tsp. lemon zest
- 1 tsp. fresh thyme leaves

**Directions:**

1. Combine the mozzarella cheese and butter in a microwave-safe bowl and microwave for 1 minute. Stir and then microwave for another minute. Stir thoroughly and allow to cool.
2. Stir in egg yolk, then stir in the almond flour to make a dough.
3. Transfer the dough to a clean, smooth surface and knead until the dough is stretchy. Shape the dough into a roll about an inch in diameter. Slice the roll into pieces about ½-inch thick.
4. Pop the dough pieces into the freezer for about 10 minutes to make them more firm.
5. Bring a large pot of water to a boil and carefully add the dumplings. Cook them for 1-2 minutes and then carefully remove them with a slotted spoon.
6. Melt the butter in a skillet, then add the thyme and lemon zest, stirring for about 2 minutes.
7. Gently add the dumplings to the pan and stir to coat with the sauce.
8. Season to taste with salt and pepper and serve hot.

**Nutrition Information Per Serving:**

- Total Fat: 55 grams
- Carbohydrates: 6 grams
- Protein: 22 grams

# *Golden Eggplant Fries*

**Servings:** 6
**Time Required:** About 60 minutes
**Ingredients:**

- 2 large eggplants
- 2 eggs
- ½ cup coconut flour
- ½ cup Parmesan cheese, grated
- ½ tsp. garlic powder
- 1/8 tsp. salt
- 1/8 tsp. pepper
- ½ tsp. parsley flakes
- ½ cup olive oil

**Directions:**

1. Peel the eggplant and cut into strips about 1 inch wide and 3 inches long.
2. Beat the 2 eggs in a small bowl.
3. Combine the Parmesan cheese, coconut flour, garlic powder, salt, pepper and parsley flakes in a medium bowl.
4. Heat the oil in a skillet over medium-high heat.
5. Dip the eggplant pieces in the egg, then dredge in the cheese mixture.
6. Fry the eggplant in the hot oil until it's golden brown, turning once to brown both sides.
7. Transfer to a paper towel to soak up excess oil, and then serve hot.

**Nutrition Information Per Serving:**

- Total Fat: 16 grams
- Carbohydrates: 5 grams
- Protein: 6 grams

# *Mashed Cauliflower*

**Servings:** 4-6
**Time Required:** About 20 minutes
**Ingredients:**

- 1 head cauliflower
- 1/8 tsp. salt
- 1/8 tsp. freshly ground black pepper
- ¼ tsp. garlic powder
- 1 cup water

**Directions:**

1. Chop the cauliflower coarsely and discard the tough core.
2. Place a steamer rack in a steamer pot and add a cup of water.
3. Place the cauliflower on top of the steamer rack.
4. Steam until the cauliflower is tender, about 15 minutes.
5. Carefully drain the water and remove the steamer rack, returning the cauliflower to the pot once it's drained.
6. If you have an immersion blender, use it to blend the cauliflower to a smooth puree, adding the seasonings as you blend. If you don't have an immersion blender, transfer the cauliflower to a blender or food processor. Optionally, you can add a tablespoon of butter as you blend for a creamier consistency.
7. Serve hot.

**Nutrition Information Per Serving:**

Total Fat: 1 gram
Carbohydrates: 5 grams
Protein: 2 grams

# *Crispy Broccoli Nuggets*

**Servings:** 4-6
**Time Required:** About 25 minutes
**Ingredients:**

- ¾ cup almond flour
- 7 Tbsp. flaxseed meal
- 4 oz. fresh broccoli
- 4 oz. mozzarella cheese
- 2 large eggs
- 2 tsp. baking powder
- Salt and pepper to taste
- ¼ cup mayonnaise
- ¼ cup fresh chopped dill
- ½ Tbsp. lemon juice

**Directions:**

1. Add broccoli to a food processor and pulse until the broccoli is ground to a meal-like consistency.
2. Combine the cheese, almond flour, flaxseed meal and baking powder with the broccoli in a large mixing bowl.
3. Add the eggs and mix well. to form a thick batter
4. Form the batter into 1-inch balls and dredge in flax seed meal.
5. Heat cooking oil in a fryer or deep skillet to 375 degrees Fahrenheit.
6. Fry the nuggets until they're golden brown, turning once to brown both side. This should take 3-5 minutes.
7. Serve hot.

**Nutrition Information Per Serving:**

- Total Fat: 8 grams
- Carbohydrates: 2 grams
- Protein: 5 grams

## *Braised Brussels Sprouts*

**Servings:** 4-6

**Time Required:** About 25 minutes

**Ingredients:**

- 4 cups Brussels sprouts, ends trimmed and cut in half
- 1 tsp. olive oil
- ½ cup water
- Salt to taste

**Directions:**

1. Heat the oil over medium-high heat in a heavy skillet. When the oil is hot, sauté the Brussels sprouts, stirring frequently, until the sprouts are beginning to brown and get crisp at the edges. This should take about 5 minutes.
2. When the sprouts are browned, carefully add the water to the pot.
3. Cover and simmer until the sprouts are tender, about 15 minutes.
4. Remove the cover and season the Brussels sprout with sea salt to taste.
5. Serve hot.

**Nutrition Information Per Serving:**

- Total Fat: 1 gram
- Carbohydrates: 8 grams
- Protein: 3 grams

## *Cheesy Stuffed Peppers*

**Servings:** 2
**Time Required:** About 60 minutes
**Ingredients:**

- 2 medium bell peppers
- 4 large eggs
- ½ cup ricotta cheese
- ½ cup shredded mozzarella
- ½ cup grated Parmesan cheese
- 1 tsp. garlic powder
- ¼ tsp. dried parsley
- ¼ cup baby spinach
- 2 Tbsp. Parmesan cheese for topping

**Directions:**

1. Pre-heat oven to 375 degrees Fahrenheit.
2. Slice the peppers in half vertically and remove the seeds.
3. Combine the cheeses, eggs, garlic powder, and parsley in a food processor and pulse until combined and smooth.
4. Spoon the egg mixture into each pepper half, stopping just below the edge. Carefully add baby spinach leaves, stirring to cover them with the egg mixture.
5. Cover the peppers with foil and bake for 35-45 minutes. The egg should be set and firm at this point.
6. Top with Parmesan cheese and place under a hot broiler for 3-5 minutes until the cheese begins to brown.

**Nutrition Information Per Serving**

- Total Fat: 16 grams
- Carbohydrates: 6 grams
- Protein: 18 grams

## *Keema Curry*

**Servings:** 4-6
**Time Required:** About 30 minutes
**Ingredients:**

- 2 Tbsp. olive oil
- 1 onion, diced
- 4 cloves garlic, minced
- 1 inch piece of fresh ginger, peeled and minced
- 1 Serrano pepper, seeded and minced
- 1 Tbsp. coriander
- 1 tsp. paprika
- 1 tsp. salt
- ½ tsp. turmeric
- ½ tsp. black pepper
- ½ tsp. garam masala
- ½ tsp. cumin powder
- ¼ teaspoon cayenne
- ¼ tsp. ground cardamom
- 1 can diced tomatoes
- 2 cups fresh or frozen peas

**Directions:**

1. Heat the oil over medium-high heat in a large skillet. When the oil is hot, sauté the onions until they are beginning to brown, about 8 minutes.
2. Add garlic, ginger, Serrano pepper, and spices, and sauté for about 1 minute more.
3. Add the tomatoes and peas to the pan, stirring to combine all the ingredients.
4. Simmer until the spices are fragrant and the sauce is bubbly, about 15 minutes.
5. Serve the curry hot.

**Nutrition Information Per Serving:**

- Total Fat: 20 grams
- Carbohydrates: 17 grams
- Protein: 30 grams

## *Savory Cake Bites*

**Servings:** 1
**Time Required:** About 10 minutes
**Ingredients:**

- 1 large egg
- 2 Tbsp. butter
- 2 Tbsp. almond flour
- ½ tsp. baking powder
- 5 tsp. sun dried tomato pesto
- 1 Tbsp. almond flour
- Salt to taste

**Directions:**

1. Combine all ingredients in a small mixing bowl and mix well.
2. Pour mixture into a microwave-safe mug.
3. Microwave on high for about 90 seconds.
4. Remove the mug from the microwave and allow to cool slightly.
5. Gently slip the cake out of the mug and serve warm.

**Nutrition Information Per Serving**

- Total Fat: 40 grams
- Carbohydrates: 5 grams
- Protein: 12 grams

## *Spicy Cauliflower Casserole*

**Servings:** 6
**Time Required:** About 40 minutes
**Ingredients:**
*For filling:*

- 1 head of cauliflower
- 2 Tbsp. heavy cream
- 1 Tbsp. butter
- ¼ cup sharp cheddar cheese, shredded
- 1 Tbsp. raw jalapenos, seeded and chopped
- ¼ tsp. garlic powder
- Salt and pepper to taste

*For middle layer:*

- 6 oz. cream cheese, softened
- ½ cup cheddar cheese, shredded
- ¼ cup salsa verde

*For topping:*

- ¾ cup colby jack cheese, shredded
- ¼ cup raw jalapenos, sliced and seeded

**Directions:**

1. Pre-heat oven to 375 degrees Fahrenheit.
2. Core and cut the cauliflower into bite-sized pieces. Place the cauliflower into a microwave-safe bowl with cream and butter. Microwave, uncovered, on high for 10 minutes. Stir well and then microwave for another 6-8 minutes.
3. Transfer the cauliflower to a blender or food processor and add cheese, jalapenos, and garlic powder. Process until the mixture is smooth, and season with salt and pepper to taste.
4. In a microwave-safe bowl, microwave the cream cheese for 30 seconds. Stir in the shredded cheese and salsa verde.
5. Spread the cauliflower puree in the bottom of a medium-size baking dish. Spread a layer of the cream cheese mixture on top of the cauliflower. Top with a layer of colby jack cheese and jalapeno slices.
6. Place in the oven and bake for 20 minutes.
7. Serve hot.

**Nutrition Information Per Serving:**

- Total Fat: 29 grams
- Carbohydrates: 4 grams
- Protein: 13 grams

## Cheesy Baked Zucchini

**Servings:** 9
**Time Required:** About 60 minutes
**Ingredients:**

- 4 cups sliced zucchini
- 1 small onion, peeled and sliced thin
- Salt and pepper to taste
- 1 ½ cups pepper jack cheese, shredded
- 2 Tbsp. butter
- ½ tsp. garlic powder
- ½ cup heavy whipping cream

**Directions:**

1. Preheat oven to 375 degrees Fahrenheit.
2. Layer a third of the sliced zucchini and onion in the bottom of a greased baking dish. Season with salt and pepper.
3. Layer ½ cup of cheese over the zucchini.
4. Repeat these steps twice with the rest of the zucchini, onion and cheese to make three layers.
5. Combine the garlic powder, butter, and heavy cream in a microwave-safe dish. Microwave for 1 minute to melt the butter and then stir well.
6. Pour the butter mixture over the vegetable and cheese in the baking dish.
7. Bake for about 45 minutes until the casserole is beginning to brown on top.
8. Serve warm.

**Nutrition Information Per Serving:**

- Total Fat: 20 grams
- Carbohydrates: 3 grams
- Protein: 8 grams

## *Coconut Cabbage*

**Servings:** 4-6
**Time Required:** About 25 minutes
**Ingredients:**

- 1 Tbsp. olive oil
- 1 medium onion, sliced
- 1 tsp. salt
- 2 cloves garlic, minced
- ½ Thai red chili, seeded and sliced
- 1 tsp. dry mustard
- 1 Tbsp. curry powder
- 1 Tbsp. turmeric powder
- 1 Asian cabbage, cored and shredded
- 1 carrot, peeled and sliced
- 2 lemon juice
- ½ cup dried unsweetened coconut, shredded
- 1/3 cup water

**Directions:**

1. Heat the oil in a large skillet over medium-high heat. When the oil is hot, sauté the onions until they are soft and translucent, about 5 minutes.
2. Add garlic, chili pepper and spices and sauté for about 30 seconds more, just until fragrant.
3. Add the cabbage, carrot, lemon juice and water, stirring to combine.
4. Simmer until the vegetable are tender, about 15 minutes.
5. Remove the cover and serve the cabbage hot as a side dish.

**Nutrition Information Per Serving:**

Total Fat: 1 gram
Carbohydrates: 6 grams
Protein: 1 gram

## *Keto Mac and Cheese*

**Servings:** 4-6
**Time Required:** About 25 minutes
**Ingredients:**

- 2 lb. frozen cauliflower florets
- 1 cup heavy whipping cream
- 4 oz. cream cheese, cubed
- 8 oz. cheddar cheese, shredded
- 1 tsp. Dijon mustard
- 1 tsp. turmeric
- ½ tsp. garlic powder
- Salt and pepper to taste

**Directions:**

1. Steam the cauliflower florets in the microwave according to the package instructions.
2. In a large sauce pan, bring the cream to a simmer. Whisk in the cream cheese and continue whisking until the mixture is smooth.
3. Stir in 6 ounces of the shredded cheddar cheese, stirring continuously until the cheese is melted.
4. Stir in the Dijon mustard, turmeric, powdered garlic, salt, and pepper.
5. Drain the cauliflower and stir it into the cheese sauce.
6. Stir in the remaining cheese and continue to stir until it is melted.

**Nutrition Information Per Serving:**

- Total Fat: 25 grams
- Carbohydrates: 5 grams
- Protein: 11 grams

# *Garlic Zucchini*

**Servings:** 4
**Time Required:** About 10 minutes
**Ingredients:**

- 2 large zucchini, peeled and coarsely grated
- 2 Tbsp. olive oil
- 2 cloves garlic, minced
- 1 tsp. lemon zest
- ½ tsp. sea salt
- 1 Tbsp. fresh lemon juice
- Salt and pepper to taste

**Directions:**

1. Heat the oil in a large skillet over medium-high heat. When the oil is hot, sauté the garlic and lemon zest just until fragrant, about 30 seconds.
2. Add the zucchini and season to taste with salt and pepper. Sprinkle lemon juice over the top of the zucchini.
3. Sauté, stirring, just until zucchini is heated through, about 2 or 3 minutes.
4. Remove from the pot and serve hot.

**Nutrition Information Per Serving:**

- Total Fat: 1 gram
- Carbohydrates: 4 grams
- Protein: 1 gram

## *Creamy Cauliflower with Cheese*

**Servings:** 4
**Time Required:** About 45 minutes
**Ingredients:**

- 2 cups cauliflower, riced
- 2 Tbsp. cream cheese
- ½ cup half and half
- ½ cup cheddar cheese, grated
- Salt and Pepper to taste

**Directions:**

1. Preheat oven to 400 degrees Fahrenheit.
2. Combine all the ingredients in a baking dish. Cover the dish with aluminum foil.
3. Place the baking dish on the oven's center rack and roast until cauliflower is tender and cheese is bubbly and beginning to brown, about 35 minutes.
4. Remove the baking dish and serve the cooked cauliflower hot.

**Nutrition Information Per Serving**

- Total Fat: 10 grams
- Carbohydrates: 4 grams
- Protein: 5 grams

## *Garlic Spaghetti Squash*

**Ingredients:**
- 1 medium spaghetti squash
- 1 cup water
- 4 cloves garlic, minced
- 1 Tbsp. olive oil
- 1 tsp. salt
- 1/8 tsp. nutmeg

**Directions:**
1. With a sharp knife, carefully cut the squash in half crosswise, across the short length of the squash instead of along the longer axis.
2. Use a metal spoon to scoop the seeds and loose flesh out of the center of both halves of the squash.
3. Place the squash halves on a baking sheet, cut side down.
4. Place the baking sheet on the oven's center rack and roast until the squash is tender, about 45-50 minutes.
5. Remove the squash and, while it's still hot, carefully shred the flesh into spaghetti-like strands with a fork.
6. Heat the oil over medium-high heat in a large skillet. When the oil is hot, add the garlic and sauté just until fragrant, about 30 seconds.
7. Toss the garlic, salt and nutmeg with the shredded squash and serve hot. For an extra kick of flavor, sprinkle with freshly grated Parmesan cheese.

**Nutrition Information Per Serving**
- Total Fat: 4 grams
- Carbohydrates: 13 grams
- Protein: 2 grams

## *Asian Eggplant Noodles*

**Servings:** 2
**Time Required:** About 25 minutes
**Ingredients:**

- 1 lb. firm tofu
- 1 cup fresh cilantro, chopped
- 3 Tbsp. rice vinegar
- 4 Tbsp. toasted sesame oil
- 2 cloves garlic, finely minced
- 1 tsp. crushed red pepper flakes
- 2 tsp. sugar-free sweetener
- 1 whole eggplant
- 1 Tbsp. olive oil
- Salt and pepper to taste
- ¼ cup sesame seeds
- ¼ cup soy sauce

**Directions:**

1. Remove the tofu from the packaging and wrap in paper towels. Place a something heavy on top and let it sit for awhile to press out most of the water.
2. Whisk ¼ cup of cilantro, rice vinegar, 2 tablespoons toasted sesame oil, minced garlic, crushed red pepper flakes, and sweetener together in a large mixing bowl.
3. Peel and cut the eggplant into matchstick-like pieces. Mix the eggplant with the marinade in the mixing bowl.
4. Heat the olive oil in a skillet over medium-low heat. Cook the eggplant in the skillet until it's soft. Add more oil if necessary to keep the eggplant from sticking.
5. Turn off the heat and cover the skillet to keep the eggplant warm.
6. Cut the tofu into 8 thick slices. Dredge the slices in the sesame seeds to coat both sides.
7. Heat the remaining sesame seed oil in another skillet and fry the tofu for about 5 minutes on each side until they're starting to get crispy. Add the soy sauce to the skillet and turn the tofu to coat. Continue cooking until the tofu is well browned.

8. Transfer the eggplant to serving plates and top with the tofu slices.
9. Serve hot.

**Nutrition Information Per Serving:**

- Total Fat: 24 grams
- Carbohydrates: 7 grams
- Protein: 11 grams

# Desserts

Do you think that when you greatly reduce the amount of carbohydrates in your diet that you say goodbye to dessert? Think again. We'll admit that coming up with decadent-seeming treats within the confines of a keto diet is a challenge, but it's a challenge we've gladly accepted. In this section, you'll find a collection of recipes that will cap off your meals in a scrumptious manner, and they'll all stay true to the goals you've st for yourself with both the keto and vegetarian diets.

# Red and Green Keto Smoothie

**Servings:** 2
**Time Required:** About 5 minutes
**Ingredients:**

- 1 ripe avocado, peeled and pitted
- 1 1/3 cup water
- 3 Tbsp. lemon juice
- 4 tsp. sugar substitute
- ½ cup frozen unsweetened raspberries

**Directions:**

1. Add all ingredients to blender.
2. Blend until smooth.
3. Divide into two equal servings in tall glasses.

**Nutrition Information Per Serving:**

- Total Fat: 20 grams
- Carbohydrates: 13 grams
- Protein: 2.5 grams

# *Pumpkin Smoothie*

**Servings:** 2
**Time Required:** About 5 minutes
**Ingredients:**

- ¼ cup pumpkin purée
- ¼ cup water
- ¼ cup vanilla whey protein
- ¼ cup sour cream
- ½ tsp. pumpkin pie spice mix
- 1 tsp. sugar substitute
- 1 Tbsp. coconut oil
- ¼ cup whipped cream

**Directions:**

1. Place all the ingredients into a blender and pulse until smooth.
2. Divide into two equal servings in tall glasses.

**Nutrition Information Per Serving:**

- Total Fat: 33 grams
- Carbohydrates: 10 grams
- Protein: 22 grams

## *Peanut Butter Smoothie*

**Servings:** 1
**Time Required:** About 5 minutes
**Ingredients:**

- ½ cup unsweetened almond milk
- ½ cup low-fat cottage cheese
- 1 Tbsp. sugar-free natural peanut butter
- 1 cup ice
- 1 tsp. sugar substitute

**Directions:**

Combine all ingredients in blender and pulse until smooth.

**Nutrition Information Per Serving:**

- Total Fat: 9 grams
- Carbohydrates: 10 grams
- Protein: 18 grams

## *Pressure Cooker Keto Cake*

**Servings:** 4
**Time Required:** About 75 minutes
**Ingredients:**

- 1 cup almond flour
- ½ cup unsweetened coconut, shredded
- 1/3 cup Stevia sweetener
- 1 tsp. baking powder
- ½ tsp. cinnamon
- 2 eggs, lightly beaten
- ¼ cup butter, melted
- ½ cup heavy whipping cream

**Directions:**

1. In a medium bowl, combine almond flour, coconut, sweetener, baking powder and cinnamon.
2. Whisk in eggs, butter and cream, one at a time, until all ingredients are well combined.
3. Pour the mixture into a pan that's small enough to fit into your electronic pressure cooker. Cover the pan with foil.
4. Place the steamer rack into the pressure cooker and pour in 2 cups of water.
5. Place the pan onto the steamer rack.
6. Cover and lock the pot.
7. Set the cook time for 40 minutes.
8. At the end of the cook time, allow the pot to vent naturally for 10 minutes.
9. After 10 minutes, carefully release any remaining steam and uncover the pot.
10. Remove the pan from the pot and allow to cool for 15 minutes. After the cake has cooled, flip the pan over and carefully encourage the cake out of the pan.

**Nutrition Information Per Serving:**

- Total Fat: 23 grams
- Carbohydrates: 5 grams
- Protein: 5 grams

# *Keto Coffee Cake*

**Servings:** 4
**Time Required:** About 70 minutes
**Ingredients:**

- 6 large eggs, separated
- 6 oz. cream cheese
- ¼ cup sugar-free sweetener
- 2 tsp. vanilla extract
- ¼ tsp. cream of tartar
- 1 ½ cups almond flour
- 1 Tbsp. cinnamon
- ¼ cup butter
- ¼ cup sugar-free maple-flavored syrup
- ¼ cup sugar-free sweetener

**Directions:**

1. Preheat your oven to 325 degrees Fahrenheit.
2. Separate the egg yolks from the egg whites. In a medium mixing bowl, cream together the egg yolks with 1/4 cup sweetener using an electric mixer.
3. Add cream cheese and mix well until a thick batter forms.
4. In another bowl, beat the egg whites with cream of tartar until they form stiff peaks.
5. Gently fold the egg whites, one half at a time, into the egg yolk mixture.
6. Gently pour the batter into a round cake pan.
7. In another mixing bowl, combine the remaining ingredients to make a stiff dough.
8. Spoon half of the dough in small dollops on top of the batter in the cake pan.
9. Bake the cake for 20 minutes, then top with the rest of the dough mixture. Return to the oven and bake for 20-30 minutes until a toothpick inserted into the center of the cake comes out clean.
10. Allow to cool before serving.

**Nutrition Information Per Serving:**

- Total Fat: 28 grams
- Carbohydrates: 4 grams
- Protein: 13 grams

# *Pressure Cooker Carrot Cake*

**Servings:** 4-6
**Time Required:** About 70 minutes
**Ingredients:**

- 3 eggs
- 1 cup almond flour
- 2/3 cup Stevia-based sweetener
- 1 tsp. baking powder
- ½ Tbsp. apple pie spice
- ¼ cup coconut oil
- ½ cup heavy cream
- 1 cup carrots, shredded
- ½ cup walnuts, chopped

**Directions:**

1. In a medium mixing bowl, mix all the ingredients using an electric mixer until the batter is well-mixed and fluffy.
2. Pour batter into a greased cake pan that's small enough to fit into your electronic pressure cooker. Cover the pan with aluminum foil.
3. Place the steamer rack in the cooker and pour in 2 cups of water.
4. Place the pan on the steamer rack.
5. Cover and lock the pot.
6. Cook at high pressure for 40 minutes.
7. At the end of the cooking cycle, allow the pot to vent naturally for 10 minutes. After 10 minutes, carefully vent any remaining pressure and uncover the pot.
8. Remove the pan from the pot and allow the cake to cool before serving.

**Nutrition Information Per Serving:**

- Total Fat: 25 grams
- Carbohydrates: 6 grams
- Protein: 6 grams

# *Keto Brownies*

**Servings:** 6
**Time Required:** About 25 minutes
**Ingredients:**

- 1 cup flaxseed meal
- ¼ cup cocoa powder
- 1 Tbsp. cinnamon
- ½ Tbsp. baking powder
- ½ tsp. salt
- 1 large egg
- 2 Tbsp. coconut oil
- ¼ cup sugar-free caramel syrup
- ½ cup pumpkin puree
- 1 tsp. vanilla extract
- 1 tsp. apple cider vinegar
- ¼ cup slivered almonds

**Directions:**

1. Pre-heat oven to 350 degrees Fahrenheit
2. Combine all the dry ingredients (flaxseed meal, cocoa powder, cinnamon, baking powder and salt) in a a large mixing bowl and whisk well to combine.
3. In a separate mixing bowl, combine the rest of the ingredients, excluding the almonds.
4. Pour the wet ingredients into the dry ingredients and mix very well with a wooden spoon.
5. Put paper muffin liners in a muffin tin and spoon approximately ¼ cup of batter into each liner. Your yield should be six muffins.
6. Sprinkle the almonds over the top of the batter, pressing them lightly into the surface so they stick.
7. Bake for about 15 minutes until the batter has risen and is set on top.

**Nutrition Information Per Serving:**

- Total Fat: 14 grams
- Carbohydrates: 4 grams
- Protein: 7 grams

# Conclusion

Our hope with this collection is that we've given you all the tools you need to use the power of the ketogenic and vegetarian diets to move you toward healthy and effective weight loss. The combination of the diets has the potential to help you achieve your weight-loss goals quickly, but you'll need a good understanding of the science behind the diets to lose weight safely and sustainably. You'll also need to be able to choose the right foods to get you to your goals.

Now that we've given you the tools, the rest is up to you. You've got everything you need to make the changes that will lead you to a healthier lifestyle. There's nothing standing in your way, and the path to a new you starts right here, right now.

18405046R00064

Made in the USA
Middletown, DE
29 November 2018